Dear Ms. Eckert,

MW01118902

care and love for
Axel. I give
God much thanks
for you!

In this joy,

Tiffany

1 Cor. 15:58

Following His Joy

Set Me Free from Anxiety

TIFFANY PAOLINI ANDERSON

Copyright © 2021 Tiffany Paolini Anderson.

All rights reserved. No part of this book may be used or reproduced by any means, graphic, electronic, or mechanical, including photocopying, recording, taping or by any information storage retrieval system without the written permission of the author except in the case of brief quotations embodied in critical articles and reviews.

This book is a work of non-fiction. Unless otherwise noted, the author and the publisher make no explicit guarantees as to the accuracy of the information contained in this book and in some cases, names of people and places have been altered to protect their privacy.

WestBow Press books may be ordered through booksellers or by contacting:

WestBow Press
A Division of Thomas Nelson & Zondervan
1663 Liberty Drive
Bloomington, IN 47403
www.westbowpress.com
844-714-3454

Because of the dynamic nature of the Internet, any web addresses or links contained in this book may have changed since publication and may no longer be valid. The views expressed in this work are solely those of the author and do not necessarily reflect the views of the publisher, and the publisher hereby disclaims any responsibility for them.

Any people depicted in stock imagery provided by Getty Images are models, and such images are being used for illustrative purposes only. Certain stock imagery © Getty Images.

ISBN: 978-1-6642-4448-1 (sc)
ISBN: 978-1-6642-4449-8 (hc)
ISBN: 978-1-6642-4447-4 (e)

Library of Congress Control Number: 2021918307

Print information available on the last page.

WestBow Press rev. date: 11/11/2021

Scripture quotations marked (NIV) are taken from the Holy Bible, New International Version®, NIV®. Copyright © 1973, 1978, 1984, 2011 by Biblica, Inc.® Used by permission of Zondervan. All rights reserved worldwide. www.zondervan.com The "NIV" and "New International Version" are trademarks registered in the United States Patent and Trademark Office by Biblica, Inc.®

Scripture quotations marked (NASB) taken from the (NASB®) New American Standard Bible®, Copyright © 1960, 1971, 1977, 1995, 2020 by The Lockman Foundation. Used by permission. All rights reserved. www.lockman.org

Scripture marked (NKJV) taken from the New King James Version®. Copyright © 1982 by Thomas Nelson. Used by permission. All rights reserved.

Scripture quotations marked (ESV) are from the ESV® Bible (The Holy Bible, English Standard Version®), copyright © 2001 by Crossway, a publishing ministry of Good News Publishers. Used by permission. All rights reserved.

Scripture marked (KJV) taken from the King James Version of the Bible.

Dedication

This book is dedicated to Ken, my husband, who wooed me into our shared forever love for our Lord and savior, Jesus Christ.

Contents

Introduction

As I lie here and type, a heating pad dressed in a pink cupcake sweater warms my weary bones. I'm twelve days past the onset of my first novel coronavirus symptom. The first day was the start of my menstrual cycle, so wanting a nap wasn't out of the ordinary. Waking to a low-grade fever was. In an instant, I realized, *I have to get tested*. That dreaded "up your nose and into your brain swab" would have to take place. My encouraging husband reminded me it could be anything. Yes, but I had had the flu vaccine, and it had been a season, really a year, where whenever something else went array, we shrugged it off and marched forward with a sigh, saying, "Because of 2020."

I was tested on the first day of December and sent home to wait in quarantine, just to be safe. I'd never heard that saying so often in all my life: just to be safe. It was like that of a parent holding a child's hand to cross the street. Now it's almost a new way of greeting someone. Bye, and stay safe! Socially distanced. Mask wearing. All very abnormal terms turned into nomenclature. So just to be safe, I had to make the hardest call: alert my aging parents, who had risked visiting over Thanksgiving from out west, that I may have been carrying the very virus we had tried so hard to protect them from. All we could do was sit and wait—and my waiting would have to be done in one of isolation from my immediate family, including our puppy. It was not the sort of first twelve days of Christmas I'd imagined spending with our three young boys. But these body-doubling joint pains are now the remnants of what's left from a rollercoaster of symptoms.

Honestly, to some degree, all parents could use a bedside staycation, where they have all their parenting power relinquished for a day—or ten. Sure, some of it has been light and fun, like hearing our youngest holler at our oversized puppy, "Scooter, stop eating the house." Some were more painful, as I overheard that same youngster's thump in the room next door as he slipped off a stair from his brother's bunk bed and broke his right arm. The only thing that held me back from storming out of my isolation room to comfort our baby were the immediate thoughts of why I was in that room to begin with. My exiting meant more exposure to possibly make him sicker. So I sat and listened as his older brothers and my husband came to the rescue. I made calls to help begin the urgent care visit for our preschooler, who was also in quarantine, just to be safe. In between these more hopeless days, it would be the outpouring of a community, even a virtual one, which would begin to refocus and restore our attention to what matters most this time of year: love in the coming of a baby in a manger, and how we felt that love. We received it in meals, calls, magazines, Lysol, toilet paper, cookies, cross-country care kits, and all of the mixed bags that this year has wrapped up to be. Hope was restored in our oldest playing Father Christmas to his younger brothers as he picked up on our Christmastime traditions, as well as the reading of *The Traveling Wise Men* by my sweet friend Chelsea Wojcik. Hope was refreshed in the neighbor's drop-off of cookie dough to host a virtual extravaganza baking session with our boys. Hope became a conviction as my isolation brought another ten thousand words to you in this book.

So where could I have possibly picked up this novel virus? Who knows? Was it in the passing of our unknowingly and later confirmed COVID-19 positive school staff, though we both wore masks and were outdoors? Was it from one of our sons who could have been asymptomatic, because the youngest cleans public windows with his tongue? Or was it the time I didn't use my hand sanitizer right after getting our groceries? I will never know. I simply know that my tough yet milder symptoms were a small price to pay. Although I lost my taste and smell from the virus meandering into my brain, so many others lost loved ones in its severe attack.

And like this more novel virus, there are diseases that attack so many of us in silent numbers. I get to type today, more than three months of being off my antidepressants, for no other reason than that of hope being restored to me. And that same hope is my story to share with you here: the hope that anxiety, panic, postpartum, depression, or any other attack you're battling will not have the last word.

So why have you picked up this book? I may never know. But the one who made this message out of my mess does. God knows. This is *His* book through *our* journey. My hope is that yours will also be restored and that whatever message you've heard up until now of not overcoming, whether decades or days in your struggle, will be met with the all-knowing power of our very real God and Jesus Christ. I hope that He will enter your space as you read what He has shared in my mess and find a new message for the story you're writing right now.

> But he said to me, "My grace is sufficient for you. My power is made perfect in weakness." Therefore, I will boast all the more gladly about my weaknesses, so that Christ's power may rest on me. That is why, for Christ's sake, I

delight in weaknesses, in insults, in hardships, in persecutions, in difficulties. For when I am weak, then I am strong. (2 Corinthians 12:9–10 NIV)

His Courtship

Spring 2001

Turning to Hollywood's leading ladies for a sense of life's direction was the beginning of my misplaced security as an only child and first-generation American from Argentine folks. I used to watch *Gentlemen Prefer Blondes* starring Jane Russell and Marilyn Monroe as my nightly routine from the wee age of seven. By my tweens, *Father of the Bride* would take over my nightly pre-dream preparations. My community college days (rather nights) showcased *My Big Fat Greek Wedding*. Yes, this eighties child made it her mission to live with these as her life truths. This would most definitely influence my black-haired roots turning blonde streaked in high school.

It was only in dating my now husband, Ken, who invited me to his church on our second date, that I would begin to form my new and true identity. He was (and still very much is) good-looking enough for me to accept this godly date and erase any "born again" preconceptions I had of him. It would not be long after that when I found myself in a pew without him. After quickly becoming a Sunday school teacher, student of whatever the Methodist Church had to offer, and joining all prayer groups, I had become what I had feared in him: a born-again Christian.

Something, or someone, was still missing. So let me start at the beginning—that is, at the beginning of how this flame was first lit. It was my very own Hollywood or Broadway show. Enter center stage: tall, light, and handsome. Ken's blond, shoulder-length locks; broad build; and deep voice had me forget all my lines. I recall dreaming up a Favio-like motorcycle entrance because one of his long locks crossed his forehead as though windswept. Later, I'd come to find out that my ride (a sweet 4Runner) was the more macho ride between the two of us—not to mention Ken's aversion to motorcycles squandering that fantasy. He was the client and architect scheduled to meet with a partner attorney and the mentor I worked with. This same mentor would use all her talents in winning this matchmaking case.

Back to my misplaced center stage. I was the receptionist and admin assistant to another one of the partners, so I was first to make his acquaintance. I quickly came to and made his presence known not only to the partner for his meeting but to all my coworkers who'd listen: the most gorgeous man I'd ever seen had just entered our premises. One by one they conveniently made their way out the front door toward the restroom to verify.

Shortly after I ushered him into his meeting with a full tray of coffee and tea fitting for Buckingham Palace, my mentor took notice. What I didn't know was later revealed by this mentor: that Ken made interrogations of his own. She supposedly had much redirection to give in that meeting from his questions about the receptionist. Once Ken left, she quickly approached my desk to confirm my interest in her client. One could say that was it for us. However, because we both were in relationships (which weren't the best for either of us), my mentor kept tabs. In fact, she also predicted our inevitable breakups with those current partners for her to unite this new partnership. And she was relentless.

My mentor confirmed a double date. Mind you—I was a freshly turned nineteen-year-old, and he was about to be thirty-four. She confirmed that he knew my age and moved on. Much, much later I would come to find out just how big of a problem our age difference really was to Ken. After having had some recent relationship hardships, a fifteen-year age gap was a no-brainer to him—and a no-go at that. So how did we end up on that double date? My mentor, the attorney. If ever in need of proper representation, her persistence pays handsomely. It turned out that as soon as she found his status was single, she began talking me up (without my knowing, as I was still struggling in my first serious relationship). Ken declined a double date several times before she was able to wear him down—or as she must have seen it, speak reason to him.

These beginnings are important. They're important to show you what lengths our relentless Father uses to seek His prodigal children and how His resources are infinite. We went out. In fact, when I arrived at our date, I had double dates. No, that is not a typo. Our double date, my mentor and her hubby, sat there, but to my surprise I didn't have just Ken there waiting. Seated with us was our local senator. No, not petitioning but partaking. He had been a previous (and unsuccessful) setup. This sweet mentor and friend was set on setting me up. The senator felt our age difference (less than mine with Ken) was an issue for his public interests. I sat at the table as if on my own episode of *The Bachelorette*. I turned and gave Ken my full attention and my business card.

He called shortly after. Our first date alone was brunch on Sunday. I hung up the phone and ran like a maniac upstairs to report to Mom. In those days, I was working full time and attending night school to secure a bachelor's degree in business. I worked for attorneys with the intent of becoming one of them until I realized the vast amount of case readings and filings required. I lived at home to pay for school. As I bounded up those stairs, I made a quick turn, missed the next step, and landed flat as can be. After popping right back up, I kept running and hollering like Cinderella after being invited to the ball. At my announcement, Mom questioned his intentions. "Sunday, huh? Wonder who his Saturday date could be?" It didn't bother me in the least. I went with it. Remember that my truths came from what Hollywood had to say. And I preferred this gentleman.

We went to the Biltmore for brunch. I went from pool halls with boys to brunch with a man. I was starstruck. I can't recall all that was eaten and talked about, except that we talked a lot. And ate a lot. For hours. I knew then that this was my dream coming true, and I would do anything to stay in that state.

Fast-forward to our second date. The church date. Funny enough, Ken picked the church based on its looks. He simply couldn't worship in a poorly designed space. I figured he took his work seriously. It was a Methodist church. He was raised Lutheran and had visited most every other denomination. He was starting to sound more normal to me. I had grown up a non-practicing Catholic, with only milestone acknowledgments, so I would not have considered myself religious. Though my mom pushed for infant baptism and communion in my elementary school age, it would be with childhood friends whose families did Sunday services or mass where I'd most take in ideas of religion. I liked their routines. I often found myself getting to spend the weekend with them so I could go. It never hurt to get a doughnut or massive cream-slobbered bagels from I Love Bagels afterward. Unlike Ken, I did not have the tradition of holiday services and hadn't attended a Bible study. That was about to change—and quickly.

At our local coffee plantation, we met weekly to study the Bible. Remember what I said about doing anything to stay in this state of dreamland? I went with it. In my mind, I was getting a coffee date. Meanwhile, Ken was pouring into a friendship to evangelize. What I didn't expect, as we read through this serendipitous study Bible that took us through books in the Old Testament, Psalms, Proverbs, and the New Testament, was the drama it would unveil. This was better than any of the movies I'd committed to memory. Prostitutes becoming heroines, brothers turning against or murdering each other, and don't get me started on Song of Solomon. We were off to a good start. I kept a journal to remind myself not to get too attached to this dream. After all, this man was the complete extreme of who I had just been with, so I thought I'd probably marry someone right in between the two. I was in control.

> There is no fear in love, but perfect love drives out fear, because fear involves punishment, and the one who fears has not been perfected in love. (1 John 4:18 NASB)

His Love

Winter 2002

Just friends. Ken had made sure I knew that was his intention. Just friends, huh? Do you kiss just a friend? One could say the journal was filling up fast with daily reminders about not getting too attached. We went out most weekends and some weeknights. First were Friday art walks and dingy, soul-searching blues or jazz music clubs on Saturdays. We often ended those nights intimately, and I started to get lost in that dream state. I decided over Christmas that because we were "just friends," I'd buy him two gifts. The first one, a country CD, would be the one I gifted if he showed up empty-handed. The second, a massage certificate, would be the "more than just friends" gift if he also showed up with one in hand. When he showed up without one, apologizing for not having anything in return, I gladly handed him the CD and smiled at the thought of getting to use the second one on myself.

These sort of self-preservation moves helped me in the short run. In the long haul, I was in need of some perspective. My sweet childhood best friend took me to her grandparents' vow renewal in northern California. I welcomed the escape. Because we're both from southern Cali, the drive up north, Thelma and Louise style, was just what I needed to unleash my heart's mess on her. After listening, she realized I had invested more in him than he may want to invest in me. During the vow renewal, the pastor shared the most provoking image that would redefine our relationship. He said, "Think of marriage with each spouse at either end of a triangle. Now look at the top. There sits God with the wife below and husband adjacent. When that happens, and those two look up toward God, the triangle reduces in size as He draws you in to close the gap between husband and wife, without any effort of their own." I was mesmerized. You mean I could look up to God, and He would fix my relationship? Done. As we headed back to the airport, I was driven by this sweet friend and her grandparents' vow renewal. I wanted to let this truth be known. I was driven to tell Ken it all. That I was done being just friends. That I was looking for the other part of my triangle. That no matter how young I was, I wasn't willing to waste another day with someone wanting to stay just friends. I had felt like a rebound and was over the dream. It was time to go back to my reality.

And like that, I told him. In my mind, we had ended whatever may had started. I couldn't get over that constant reminder, as though I didn't merit his acknowledgment of anything further. Well, I wasn't going any further. And I do believe that through the journaling, through my going to my friend's grandparents' vow renewals, God was watching over me and guiding me. My not acknowledging him outright as Lord and Savior was limited from a total misunderstanding. Given the priestly examples I had while growing up, I thought of Jesus like a brother relationship where He represented a barrier in my having direct access with His Father, my God. I had no idea that Jesus, the Son of God, was God! More to come on that confession.

This walking out on a friendship with Ken lasted but a day. The next day, I received an email. The closest thing we had to smartphones were pagers, and typing hello in numbers upside down was as sophisticated as it got. The email asked for a coffee date. Later that afternoon, Ken asked us to be exclusive. I had a boyfriend. No longer just friends!

> God is within her, she will not fall; God will help her at break of day. (Psalm 46:5 NIV)

His Timing

Winter 2003

Yes, a year passed, and many sweet moments were shared. It took Ken six months once we were exclusive to say, "I love you." To this day, it is a rarity to hear, yet it is remarkable when done. A trip to visit with friends in San Francisco for my birthday. Hikes with those same friends through Sedona. And a lot more first Fridays and second Saturdays to tell about. It was better than my dreams. It was my reality. Until ... a friend from our then church—because we were now avid Sunday goers too—had asked me on a ladies' spiritual weekend retreat. I was timid about it. A weekend away with already spiritually primed women wanting me to divulge an honest walk with God that I wasn't confident in was just a bit too much. At Ken's prompting, I went. God really can use anything, or anyone.

A walk to Emmaus. Out of respect for what that walk holds dear and near to those who plan to attend, I won't divulge much. I will say that my concerns were realized as I asked one of the lead teachers Friday night to be released early and go home. I simply wasn't connecting. She implored me to reconsider and give it to Saturday morning. Wouldn't you know it? That was the message I needed to hear. God incarnate speaking through the flesh of the woman before me the next morning, giving me conviction of a new life I had never explored. I prayed more those next two days than in my twenty years. I don't mean rattling off names out of superstition that unless I pray for my loved ones, something ill-fated would happen. I mean the kind of prayer that was two-way. I was quiet. I was listening. I was in love—not with Ken but with God, with Jesus. With being free from the love of man. I may have taken it too literally. I once again marched up to Ken after the retreat to give him a piece of my "not wasting any more time" talks. If he wasn't ready to commit, I wasn't willing to wait around. I can see his "here we go again" expression on his face like it was yesterday.

I later came to find out that my friend who referred me to the retreat had had this same "coming to Jesus" ultimatum with her own hubby. That would've been a good warning beforehand. I will never forget Ken's response. "You don't want me to ask right here, right now, do you?" Of course not. I didn't want to make him. But wasn't I? I was on fire. The flame was lit, and I had a God to serve—with or without a man. I was determined.

Not more than a month later, I boarded a plane with Ken and a rose in hand to Pacific Beach, California. My happy place. Really, any beach is my happy place. I had a month to think, a month to stay in our relationship. And to be truthful, I had a month to forget all about a marriage proposal. Even with the rose in hand, it was the last thing on my mind. That might be the power of the salty air for me. I was simply grateful to lie like a clam and bake all day. So when he interrupted those plans on our weekend getaway for a camera, one he had to purchase immediately, I was indignant. He claimed to have forgotten his. We walked across to the local Rite-Aid, but none were good enough. He said something about needing it to take streetscape pictures for work. The only real barometer I had for architecture was with my former and first boyfriend, who had been striving to become an architect. In my attempt to "fix his life" and guide him into that career, it led me into my own. I would become the better candidate for going to the school I was pushing him to apply for, and I'd later graduate from it as a business major. As I spent time with Ken, who needed none of my doing or pushing, just my encouragement, it became a reminder of this adult relationship. Out of my willingness to support him and his work dreams, I boarded that dingy bus for an hour-long ride into the city to find just the right camera with just the right lens.

This had to stop. We only had one more day on those sandy fronts. So when we returned to sunset and he changed into his nice clothes only to usher me out with him for just the right picture on the local pier, I was still none the wiser. After running for this perfect picture, which had changed from streetscape to a sunset, I had just about had it. When we arrived pierside with only a few couples left because this private pier was closing, he decided the lighting was all wrong and walked away. I turned to face those waves and prayed, "Lord, give me patience as I'm now done with this man." In that moment, Ken returned to talk about the moment. Something about making moments last. I interrupted him to give him my latest NPR report that spoke to that very topic. He quickly quieted me and proceeded to ask. Well, you know. Let's say I'm not sure I heard the question simply out of confusion in seeing that brilliant box open to a greater brilliance from that stone. As he was about to ask me to marry him again, I said yes!

The next morning, our last on the beach, I had a chance for me to take it in alone as Ken slept in. I had a chance to journal, stretch, and pray. At the beachside I was almost alone. I was interrupted by two young Latinos who could've seemed precarious (not in talking to this Latina, but just in their boldness to approach me as a complete stranger), but they turned out angelic. They asked if I often came here to do this very thing. I said it was a first, and I also showed the other first: a ring I now wore proudly as a newly engaged. They smiled. Then the most peculiar part came when they spoke, almost in command, that I never stop taking this time for myself and for God. As I gazed down to look at what this ring and new chapter in my life would mean, and before I could thank either one of them, they left. No, they had disappeared. The beach was practically empty in that early hour, and their whereabouts would have taken time to walk away. I chose to accept that heavenly gift of wisdom: to prioritize God time, self-care, and other care. Though I'd have to learn this again and again. I did come to learn one of the young man's names was Angel, and so he was.

> But you have come to Mount Zion, to the city of the living God, the heavenly Jerusalem. You have come to thousands upon thousands of angels in joyful assembly. (Hebrews 12:22 NIV)

His Forgiveness

Spring 2004

Nudges. I've rewritten this part more times than I will ever confess. I still struggle to recollect. It was our wedding day. The day itself, outside of the flood watch in the foothills of a desert oasis, was spectacular. The wedding to the man of my dreams was a real dream come true. The reception was so festive, I can still smile at the joy that was had by all, including this bride. What pangs me to recollect are the nudges.

A nudge the morning of the day when I arose to journal, stretch, and pray—only to realize how infrequently I'd done so during the entire year's worth of preparations. Oh, many preparations were of the logistics, just not of the heart. What had happened to the girl beachside, touched by an angel? Well, I'd given in to the plans, and not mostly my own but the plans of others. I did not want to offend others and sought to please my groom, our parents, the bridal party, and the 350-plus growing guest list. I was so lost in the details that I made no room for what mattered to me or to God.

I had seen a picture-perfect dress way out of my budget. Though the party cost us the same as our down payment on our home, I couldn't justify asking for what my heart fancied. I dismissed it as being selfish. It was a price tag my parents couldn't and shouldn't have to afford. I now know this was masked as false humility. Always go for the dress, ladies. This was simply one of the many cuts I took for our wedding. What I needed was to cut the diva hairstylist and makeup artist, who had me in tears over my late arrival. My tardiness came from a seating arrangement I pored over in hopes of not offending a soul, and ultimately my maid of honor's beau would take over to finalize the weekend of this affair. I was grateful for his willingness, especially because her boyfriend had just met me the weekend of our nuptial exchange and was reorganizing the seating chart to squeeze every last body in. No wonder my boss was livid for being placed on the far side of the library. Yes, the library. This event was multifaceted and the first of its kind. With my architect's dream to party in a unique space, we settled and pioneered the first ever wedding reception in the Downtown Phoenix Burton Barr Public Library, filled with glass elevators lifted above a small indoor pool of water. It was a striking setting after the preparty down the road at a friend's art studio with martinis sliding down the ice luge. Not to mention the postparty carnival when the clock struck midnight. The details had many hands and required even more.

When the morning of this blessed affair arrived, something was off. With so many details swirling in my mind, I knew better than to stay put. I was being nudged, being called to go take one last ride. No, not to escape the blessed marriage. It was the kind of ride that can only be done on horseback. I'd had Bailey, my white Arabian horse, since our family had relocated to Arizona. That morning, I had this great desire to ride him. Instead, I followed orders and cannot even recall what preparations I lost myself in. The day afterward, I got a call from my horse trainer and beloved friend that she had completely forgotten the date of our wedding. God's nudge to rise and ride was also for relationship, to remind my sweet friend to come celebrate with us. Instead, I aimed to please and missed the message.

The greatest nudge of all were the morning calls to come and worship, to be at the feet of my good God who just wanted my time, like a dad wanting a daughter's attention. When my earthly father walked me down that aisle, I was confessing to my heavenly one for the neglect. Like a bad rollercoaster I could not exit, I walked toward that cross in our modern church sanctuary, confessing—no, imploring that God forgive me neglecting Him. That He still blessed us and me. That He would help me choose Him more. I was a mess. The man of my dreams stood before me, and I felt so far from him with my eyes taken off our headship. There was nothing Ken could do or say to me, or any outward beauty that would satisfy my indwelling need of God's love. This very joyous day would not be made complete without Him. Of course, God embraced me down that aisle. It would take years for me to embrace Him back, unveiled and unashamed. Instead, I walked toward our pastor as he asked if I'd like to lift my veil during the service. I again chose false humility and the stuff of movies to keep it covered, veiling my shame.

> And we all, with unveiled face, beholding the glory of the Lord, are being transformed into the same image from one degree of glory to another. For this comes from the Lord who is the Spirit. (2 Corinthians 3:18 NIV)

His Word

Summer 2005

A year into our happily ever after, I still kept my nightly rituals of the same movie before bed. Well, I had graduated to *Runaway Bride*, which was safe enough given my marital status being locked in. Halfway through, I began to be pulled back to reality. My body had begun to have some sort of reaction. Without my thinking, because I was pretty distracted by the horse and bride on the screen, my legs and arms began shaking through no desire or making of my own. Had I instantly become diabetic? My naivety would continue. I hollered Ken into our bedroom and asked that he sweep me to the closest emergency room. My poor husband. Side note: that first year's novelty of saying *husband* was one of my greatest thrills. This protector-of-all figure was now my protector. Little did he know what he had signed up for with the "in sickness and in health" part of our contract.

We arrived to sit and wait. The shaking was steady. I observed my legs with such confusion. I wasn't telling them to make this maneuver. What disease could be taking over my twenty-four-year-old frame? I worked out, slept well, and ate decent. Finally I was ushered into the array of tests, and it was official. The physician came to his conclusion: "Just find your happy place." Excuse me? What did he just tell me to do? It was like a bad episode of *ER*. Yes, I had just had my very first (of many) official panic attack.

We drove home. Bewilderment described both of our states—mine for having caused what seemed like an uncontrollable state, his for not really knowing what he signed up for. Sadly, this would be just the beginning of many episodes and evolutions to follow. Most of my future attacks would attack me when out at night, all dolled up. I would have irrational thoughts of being slipped some foreign substance in a drink, as though I was some sort of sought-after Russian spy. I knew I needed professional help. I knew Ken deserved a wife he could enjoy outside of the home. Though we still continued our outings, most nights ended in panic. There was one effective antidote. A friend had shared several scripture verses with me, telling me to memorize them like lines for a show. My mind rehearsed them like my life depended on it because it felt that real. "For God has not given us a spirit of timidity, but of power and of love and of a sound mind" (2 Timothy 1:7 NKJV). I found myself rehearsing this one scripture over my shakes, and it would help subside them after a good fifteen minutes. This seemed to be the only method that would eventually lessen the symptom.

What was my symptom of? Not wanting to adopt any labels, I did seek alternate care. Clean eating, power yoga, dance therapy—you name it. The dance would be a real comfort for me, both for the therapy and the friendship found in this family friend, dubbed my second mother, remaining behind the scenes for most of my life. As my dance therapist, she would push me to dance out my emotions. This led to many dance improvisation sessions. Where I would play a random song and have no choreographed movement. Rather would be propelled to move from the rhythms of the song. As a struggling dancer who had hoped to co-choreograph the Oscars alongside Debbie Allen, I struggled not for lack of desire but of talent, or so I would be told. It turns out my feet turnout will always be improper for their high arches. This is something my now dance therapist and I shared. Her dreams for formal ballet training would be rejected due to her overall slender height. Instead, she turned me toward her more modern expression of dance and life. So how could this "in tune with her body" girl become so out of tune with her body now? No amount of dancing would expose what only my good God could show me—when I was ready. And I was too in control for Him to take any wheel.

> Fear not, for I am with you; be not dismayed, for I am your God; I will strengthen you, I will help you, I will uphold you with my righteous right hand. (Isaiah 41:10 ESV)

His Face

Summer 2006

It had been a year in this new role as wife, where Ken and I lived in a historic home in downtown Phoenix. I came to love it for its charm and unknowing preparations of our future East coast living. This 1930s English Tudor home was placed in a historic neighborhood off one of the highest using meth streets. Although its roots were founded in farming, it had turned into an eclectic and even daring way to live. Needless to say, when the local pizzeria closed down for adding more than what one paid for in their toppings, this didn't sit well for my already panic-driven thoughts. But to drive down its palm tree–lined road was the sweetest of homes for us. It was barely over a thousand square feet, so Ken and I lived in a tiny home compared to most of our church friends' three-thousand-square-feet mega homes, uphill in Paradise Valley. Their houses may have been set apart, but their open-home gatherings and invites left for no divide. These kinds of folks would soon become an extended part of our family.

My actual family lived thirty minutes away, but this was still really my first year on my own. Though married and working, I recall the sense of freedom I had because Ken had been, and still remained, so independent. Some shy from marriage due to the commitment. As an only child and daughter, I had just found myself. I could think, be, and do as I please. There were no curfews or asking for permission, though I would often turn to Ken as a father figure in need of his approval over my whereabouts. I wanted nothing to do with the freedom some seek in late-night outings, drunken stupor, or other forms of rebellion, all of which I had sampled. Instead, it was the sort of freedom stemming from adulthood, whether it was what I wanted to cook, or not cook at all, or the places in the world I still wanted to see.

That freedom may have been established physically, but mentally I was still struggling. A very real codependence existed with my mother. Even physically, Mom had welcomed herself into our new bungalow. And with fresh laundry and meals prepped, I slowly became trained again into our old way of life. I was a daughter to a mother who still mothered, and often. Here I was, a grown married woman, being cared for by her mother. Ken didn't mind, so we let it grow. One meal soon became most dinners. And it wasn't for lack of Mom's own busyness. As a radio personality and media guru, mom was more than involved among the elitist of circles. That also turned into many open doors for Ken and me professionally, from mayors to governors and wealthy entrepreneurs. We very much enjoyed a lifestyle of this ease.

It was in work where I grew the most—not my nine-to-five work but the dishes, folding, and gardening. When Ken traveled, I saw it as a time of refuge to learn what it was like to be alone. Strangely enough, as an only daughter, I may have been alone in not having a healthy dose of sibling rivalry, but not in other maturing ways. So much attention came to me in the way of future plans and present perfect manners. My performances were often even highlighted, thanks to Mom's contributions. One morning at the local bagel shop, Ken and I were asked by the cashier if we were indeed *the* Ken and Tiffany. She had just seen our recent engagement pictures and then wedding celebration images in the local Spanish paper. This attention would make for fun, but it also carried its own pressures. One day the pressure would tip over into more of an explosion.

On one of Ken's trips, my folks came for a visit. It was another warm, sunny afternoon in the Valley of the Sun. Mom would remind me to be sure to clean the house thoroughly before Ken's return, all while cooking us a meal and getting my laundry going. Her unsolicited advice was untimely. I began to raise my voice, though I was not certain why I needed to be so upset over the help. Really, it was more of a desire to be seen and respected as the adult I was trying to become. Mom's example from her mother was no better. Having had my grandparents split when she was a young teen, Mom's upbringing was far from ideal. I knew this, in theory. Played out in real life, I struggled with allowing her control to not affect my response. In that heated minute, I screamed so loudly for them, both dad and mom, to vacate the premises immediately. In what would have been a usual cold response from me to simply ignore the battering, I had lost it. Asking your parents to exit while stomping like you're having a toddler tantrum is anything but adult. Yet it was for my own self-preservation, because my body shut down and clammed up in bed after they left. I felt all the drudgery of my actions, a common loop I played from her underhanded remarks and my oversensitivity, and I turned to something different. Someone different.

I often relied on friends to coax me through hardships, or even Ken. This time I turned inward. While lying in a pool of my own tears, the thought of seeking His face from the Bible came to mind. "Seek my face," I recall reading. I wanted so badly to not really be alone, so I kept my eyes sealed tight. The back of my eyelids remained a place of darkness as I searched for a face I'd never met. All of a sudden, like a kid building a Lite Brite design in billboard lighting, I began to see the outline of a man's face. Those lights lit up a very real outline of a man I'd never met. I was dazed and confused, wondering whether I was dreaming this up in my mind. I also felt a need to pay attention. It was as though a different world was being opened to me. And in those lights, in His warmth, I slept until morning came.

I was amazed at how well I slept given such a jarring night. That would have normally required many hours to unwind from with heavy dosing of a migraine med. I realized I was not visited by some fictional presence like that of the ghost of Christmas past but by the very real Holy Ghost of the present. And it was indeed a present—not that I received a sound night's rest, but to know I was being cared for in such a real way by someone so real in His own way. At the same time, I knew enough to know we are not to go it alone. I eventually told Ken and sought help from pastoral staff at our church to understand my struggle. It was surprising, and yet not, to hear that the relationship between Mother and me had been one of manipulation and emotional abuse. Given Mom's own physical and emotional abuse, I was thankful to only have one fruit fall from that tree.

My church family stepped up. I would go on to have friends take me to lunch and talk through their own spiritual walks. Their testimonies were so hopeful. They seemed to be functioning and even thriving after such hardships. One friend shared that Christian music was her saving grace. Having embraced most all genres, from country to tango, that was one I had not ventured into, mainly for the thought of it not being as relevant. On this early morning driving into work off the I-17 normal route into work, among the traffic, I tuned into the local Family Life Radio on 90.3 FM, and that's when I heard it. Simple lyrics done with a haunting voice that reminded me of my beloved alternative rock days. Jeremy

Camp was the name of the artist, and "Give Me Jesus" was the song. I was hooked.

I began to attend prayer gatherings in the homes of these church friends. The idea of praying in front of others, as a people pleaser, was debilitating. Would I say the right thing? As if there is a right thing. Insecurities loomed over what felt like wearing the wrong sized shoe. I stumbled. Instead of getting back up, I'd lose hope in ever having what these friends deemed as a real relationship with a living God. Even after my encounter with his lit-up face, I doubted. What did He sound like? How many candles would I have to light, or what direction would I face, for Him to hear me? Their challenge to me: Go take a hike.

I'll never forget that sweet friend who looked upon my state of confusion with prayer and laughed. She redirected me into nature. Another friend said to simply sit still. One morning I did both. As I sat at our green-painted, single-paned window, I looked out on the morning's dew. Even in the middle of the Valley of the Sun, the birds made their way to the brightly colored nectar found in most cacti flowers. Our particular front scape carried Ocotillo with red flowers that happened to have a hummingbird this morning. I was amazed at their flight speed, which looked frozen in time, and I stared as it had its morning drink. As quickly as it came, it left. I stayed resting my chin near the windowpane when in an instant, it was back. This time we were eye to bird eye. I stared at this magnificent creature in its flight. Like a dream, I counted the seconds of the stare-off as it hummed in a circle right at my nose with a single pane separating us. Thirty seconds later, it took off for its new flight. I was left enamored. How could this tiny creature and I have just exchanged more than mere glances?

Since that moment, hummingbirds are commonplace for me when I'm in need, in prayer, or even in recounting with a friend. That is exactly what happened with a sweet friend's visit. Upon sharing my exchange, we had a hummingbird sweep past us both, as though God were simply showing off His resources. Then there was the time my mom and I had needed the comfort, and she pointed to one out in front of the car windshield hovering over us. I now take these little bird friends to be God moments and an answer to my pondering how God shows up. Oh, He shows up—and He often shows off. I'm simply not always in tune. When we do turn up the God volume, our Creator uses His creation to create an intimate moment with whomever will seek Him. Unlike the prince in this world, He won't barge in. He'll remain gentle as He knocks on the door of your heart.

> Ask and it will be given to you; seek and you will find, knock and the door will be opened to you. (Matthew 7:7 NASB)

His Leading

Fall 2007

New job, same business. But I had no business being there. That was what sank my high-heeled step down the cubicle-lined hallway. I knew better than to keep walking. I would take my seat and swivel to the computer before me. I had gone to great lengths to find and relocate myself here. I was now in control, I told myself. While Ken remained loyal despite any leadership hardships at work, I had ventured into my now third employer. I also told myself the main difference was him being in a career—a passionate one, and a second one at that. How many people get to live out two professions they're talented in and thrive? First, Ken was a professional tennis player, which I wouldn't have discovered had it not been for his mother's ability to clip and save every article and picture related to this first calling. Having stopped after reaching around the top thousand in the world while playing on the European circuit, he would extend his pro time in this sport as coach and hitting partner to a then popular young tennis star, Kathy Rinaldi.

Ken then headed off for his master's in his new passion and practice of architecture. As an architect, he has been dogmatically successful. His drive to be consistent in all he did to both study and pass those umpteen tests for his official license overwhelmed me. His work ethic was like that of my father's. My mother's success came from always stirring her profound soup bowl of projects. It was not unusual for those in the arts to do a little of everything. But Dad, well, to this day he has over fifty years in his plastic manufacturing business, no matter the competition that would drive him out of that work. He works for days on end, never tiring of his Monday to Friday schedule near LA, where his La-Z-Boy chair in his office is his weeknight bed. After returning to Phoenix only for a weekend retreat, he would then repeat it all again come Monday morning. This sort of work ethic wasn't the one I would adopt. I would get the more creative, and sometimes fleeting, approach, like that of my mother.

It would be the dreams and beliefs of my parents that I'd truly adopt, such as becoming a successful corporate attorney, because those received more compensation, Dad would counsel. Or I could be a high-up politician to one day change the world as our first Latina president, Mom would urge. Both of those doors closed on me, or I closed them. I dangled from one notion to the next, never really taking time to see my own interests and abilities. As I took my seat in front of this now new task, the only honor was in those I served, because this was a company solely focused on our military's health care. Given my background in some brief politics, and that of the arts through Mom, I never cowered at the notion of engaging with any of our top executives. That quickly led me into a fanciful world to staff our company's top execs in countless events, often involving Hollywood patriots. Though I accepted this calling, I was far from hearing my calling.

The closest I came to having a calling all of my own was before taking on this role, I made it a point to do some adulting. I traveled alone—well, almost alone. An older couple in our church had offered their getaway place on the Mayan Riviera in Mexico. Ken was a bit concerned. He was without any vacation time, and I was in between jobs. My desire to go it alone definitely raised his brow. I assured him this was part of my figuring things out as an adult. Having traveled the world alongside my parents as a child left me wanting for more as an adult. Therefore I took up the offer of this sweet elderly couple to hitch a ride, and I packed my bags.

I had often been to Mexico, so this was not so much for the scenery as it was for the independence of traveling to have new experiences. I was already very content in my marriage, and I had no distractions about seeking a romantic interest, though I did call home to report one love interest: that of Angel, with whom I got to have a ride. Angel the dolphin would become an adventure I'd long carry into my adulthood, with my future children doting on these pictures. Though our trip started with fun and games, it made a turn for the more serious. This elderly couple soon became my personal tour guide into the beauty found on the other side of the highway.

There's one main highway that takes you to most resorts on the Mayan Riviera from the airport in Cancun, Mexico. Headed south, you make a left into a world of entertainment, dining, and private residences to live the "good life." Take a right, and that gets you right into the heart of the Mayan people. It turns out this couple had not only invested their time and resources into the local communities but also befriended so many of the locals. I was taken to visit the village that was being built by the local government on the other side of this main highway. These new dwellings held no doors, but they had hung hammocks in the main bedrooms. No windows would allow the removed ocean breezes in for a sort of natural air-conditioning. The local school had no library, and this sweet couple made it their mission to equip them with one.

Then we headed farther inland to visit one of the more

recent unearthed Mayan ruins, but not without first taking a side stop. At this point, I was far from surprised as this couple recounted so many adventures, including that of turtle surfing off the coast. I followed suit. As we pulled over to a nondescript local shop that sold handmade blankets and trinkets, I didn't think much of it. It was typical to tourists from the front, but we were quickly embraced by the local shop owner. It turned out a friendship had been developed over the years with my tour guides. We were ushered behind the shop's curtains and were welcomed into this shop owner's humble abode. Their home consisted of dirt floors, a straw roof, and many open-to-the-sky areas. Grandma was kneading with her hands some masa while the beans cooked in a pot over a small fire. Children ran around with much joy while chasing their pet, a pig. The smiles on every person in that household was warm and welcoming. There was a joy so simple and radiant, it was hard not to join in it. So we did. We ate and laughed alongside them. No next stop could ever compare or has since.

When we did return to their private quarters, I took in the luxury and realized the isolation that could quickly come with it. I chose to sleep with the windows open that night, in honor and inspired by those I came to meet. It might have been 4:00 a.m., but I was unsure given the darkness still out. I awoke to a song—not a chirping, though it was of birds, but of singing. These melodic birds were so captivating, and I recorded their tunes to bring home and share. I stayed up being serenaded and realized this melody was from the Creator. It was a gentle leading into the quiet time of prayer. This sort of worship was a way to connect with Him, so I did. We remained more connected on that getaway than ever before. That was why I wasn't totally surprised that upon my return to entering those new office doors, I wasn't called to be there. Some would call it a sort of intuition, but I started to call it my God. He was trying to warn me to wait, to not go before him, and to listen. I had done the opposite. But in His goodness and mercy, He would use even this for His and my good plans. I walked in them and with Him, and I would have to wait some more before being called again. This time, I'd obey.

> We know in all things God works for good with those who love him. Those he has called according to His purpose. (Romans 8:28 NIV)

His Goodness

Winter 2008

In the wake of early 2008, Ken and I would stand to lose a small fortune. We had just purchased our dream lot for an original home to be designed by Ken. This surely had to be God's calling. I even made a vision board. I would drive into the private gated community to dream up our cul-de-sac living in our one-of-a-kind modern home. This was purchased after the successful sale of Ken's DC row house flip. We did not see ourselves back east anytime soon, but in reality we'd be moving back there in a few years' time. We decided to invest in over a handful of properties near us in downtown Phoenix. Our hopes were to have that same beautification effect that Ken was able to make on R and 7th Street in DC. So with those profits, we invested—not into a larger, greater home for ourselves, which would have made for an easier future sale, but with fixer-uppers and vacant land to ultimately build our own dream home.

When we took our plans to permit in late 2007, never could we have imagined having a recession greet us in the New Year. There were no construction loans to be secured and no private investors to co-build with us. There was no new, one-of-a-kind home to live in anytime soon. Our dreams were crushed, and our reality grew even more gruesome. All the fixer-uppers were just that, in need of fixing up. We hadn't accounted for the cost to do so. We would be led to evict tenants for their lack of payments, including one while incarcerated. That may have been the awakening of the slumlord living that I wanted us out of. We would later go on to have two short sales and one foreclosure in the span of just a few years. This led to a reality of being blacklisted from almost all near future investments or opportunities. It would even come into questioning our character, given the security clearance needed in my new role at work. As though we were in a court of law, a prosecution-like interview process required countless documents and logs of communications to the mortgage lenders, in hopes of showing our good-faith efforts to have not been foreclosed on. Our finances were upside down, and so was our marriage.

In the midst of this, we were blessed to be pregnant with our first child in a much more uncertain future. We had not counted the costs, though we thought otherwise. Ken deliberates over any decision for extended periods of time—which is nothing like my impulses. I too had wanted this for us. Being married to an architect who could design our very own dream home was a dream come true, and I made it my business to push for this dream against God's will. Never did I pray about this major life investment. Instead, I took on the phenomena of creating my own vision board to have willed this property and future home build into existence. Had I only known. We would eventually move back east. We would never build what we had dreamed up. This vacant land would take more than a decade of paying tens of thousands a year to sell. Had I known all of this, I would have never pushed for what I thought we wanted. Yet God knows all we need. He knows what all needs are, be it the birds in the sky or the lilies on the ground. Both are cared for perfectly. That's why He warns us to seek first His will, His kingdom, and His love for us. We must trust He will take care of it all—what we'll wear, what we'll eat, and even where we'll live.

Though we were tense, cold, and often short with each other, I didn't question our marriage. However, we both lacked grace for one another out of our surprise and sadness to lose so much of what we had invested in. Therefore when we had the chance to go out to dinner on my company's bill, we took it. It was our company party, so we could get gussied up at another's expense. We almost could forget about the mess we had financially placed ourselves in, and we took a break. Before entering the ballroom, Ken held me back to apologize. He confessed his needing to have known better, especially given our age difference. He laid it on his shoulders alone. That moment opened up our marriage to choose it over our circumstances. Money would still go on to be a sore point in our marriage, but in that moment he was choosing us. I quickly assured him of our shared mistake and how sad I was to have pushed us so hard with what I thought was the next right step. I had thought, "If I'm married to an architect, then we should live in his design!" Knowing we both wanted our marriage to remain intact gave us a common ground to rebuild. It would be a long life lesson to learn from, going paycheck to paycheck, with many closed financial doors given our poor choices.

The next day, I was able to meet up with a girlfriend for her favorite iced tea drink while I spilled most of what had happened in search of the root of our issues—or rather, my issue. Why had I been so blinded to not see how this would put our future family in such a mess? Her reply floored me. She said my problem was pride. I honestly thought she was wrong. That ought to have been my first confirmation of having this problem. Instead, I thought of how I was constantly told how hard I was on myself. I was already dealing with a perfection and performance mindset, so I didn't need to add this third *P* word in my life. And how on earth did I struggle with pride when I put others' needs before myself, or so I thought? It bothered me for days. No, scratch that—it still puts me in check years later. How did I have a pride problem? Well, not admitting it was my first clue. If I didn't have pride issues, then a quick self-reflection would have countered that. Then there was false humility, this idea that poor me was in play over anything that happened to me. Yes, it was rooted in insecurity, and I'd often do anything for others at the expense of my well-being. This mindset to work for the affirmation of others in any way possible left me no other choice but to see the pride that did indeed lie before me. It would be the first of many steps in shedding this ugly truth.

> But don't begin until you count the cost. (Luke 14:28 NASB)

His Calling

Winter 2009

Winter, if one could call it that in the Valley of the Sun, was anything but cold. Well, at least not at sun height. The nights were a different story. Cold enough to get down to freezing temperatures. This particular Sunday morning was anything but frigid. I wore a loose-fitting floral dress as we drove up to our church in Paradise Valley. The name is not a metaphor. We first went to our class that dubbed itself as home improvement. We were one of the younger couples, just beginning our parenting adventures as I sat seven months pregnant that January morning. Our firstborn was not due for a couple of months. We sat there with this growing blessing inside of me, confident that the time for us to parent would be such a great calling. After all, we had followed our (or rather Ken's) five-year plan to wait on kids. And he was right: that afforded us the time to simply be us. He was wiser in his years, and I followed suit.

We traveled to where his first career took place in the German countryside. He whisked me off to the epitome of romantic settings, Prague. And how could it not be, with the mountainside hotel that offered us gondola rides to our room and roses in our toilets? It was truly unique. It was a city of romance in the air and across the cobblestone, and it offered us both a greater appreciation for the other. When the blessed news came of our soon to be growing family, my mother hosted a wedding-sized baby shower, with DJ and all. Our church was gracious to host our no-booze afternoon affair. And no alcohol was needed with the Latin side ripping it up on the dance floor; this baby and I proudly partook in it. All of this is to say we felt ready—just not that ready.

Back to this sunny Sunday morning. I leaned over to my sweet friend and asked, "Do you recall sneezing and dripping?" What I meant was it wasn't unusual for the slightest cough or sneeze to send me to the restroom in hopes to catch the rest of the mess.

She looked at me and said, "Well, sure." Oh good, a typical symptom. As a first-time mom, anything out of the ordinary, which was everything these days, sent me into twenty-one questions of friends who could offer insight into my endless thoughts. But just to be sure, she suggested I go clean up and quickly went into the sanctuary—not to offer up any prayers but to solicit the help of her mother sitting and contemplating in a church pew, because a service ran at the same time as our class. Her mom happened to be a labor and delivery nurse and a lactation consultant for the same hospital where we were expected to have our baby. When I heard my friend's mom ask certain vital questions at the door of the restroom, I didn't think much of it. That is, until she propped open the door and hollered, "Ken, go get the car now."

What had I said? Which of my responses made her think this was an emergency? I'd learned to stay padded these days given this common occurrence. Forgive the details, but I later learned it was the smell of my swift accident that was alarming. It was as though this was a different sort of liquid my body was creating. Ken and I can now laugh at that then alarming ride to the emergency room. In fact, he later confessed his worry over my ruining the passenger-side leather seat. Meanwhile, I lived in denial that our baby was coming. It was nearly two months too early, and I hadn't found the right shade of green for the nursery. My nesting instincts had only begun to kick in. We didn't want to find out the gender of our baby until the big day, so green was the perfect neutral base. Funnily enough, green would come to be the favorite color of our sweet babe.

The nurse asked a few questions before checking whether there was any dilation. Five centimeters. She announced, "You're having this baby today." Wait, what? No! That was not possible. We were nowhere near our due date. And what about my doula? And where was my birth plan? Oh, I was ready in that respect. I had complete control over this birth. I'd convinced Ken to enroll in hypnobirthing, just one of the many ways we women prepare ourselves for birthing. And clean-eating me was convinced of a natural childbirth. Don't laugh; I'm sure you had thoughts of this lofty goal too. Some of you even met it multiple times. Well, I was determined. Just not this early.

Ken called our friends from church and family. What would this mean? A baby born this early? The specialist team was then introduced. A team of neonatologists (which would take me the entire stay to finally learn how to say that) and NICU nurses came to give their introductions. Our baby would come to live in their world after entering it. They had to give me this steroid in hopes to develop the baby's lungs to breathe on its own. And we really needed a second dose before the baby's birth to ensure proper breathing. The problem lay in that the second dose would need to take place after forty-eight hours.

We prayed, we shared, and the church family answered. Their prayers were met with an amazing response. Miraculously, later that Sunday, my contractions ceased. Baby's vitals were strong, and I would lie in bed for a couple more days in hopes for the second steroid dose to develop our baby's lungs.

The medical team was leery and ready. I later found out that a C-section rolling bed was outside my room at all times; this was their practice given my situation. My circle of influence was not only church but also my dear friends from the yoga world. In fact, my yoga instructor was also our doula. She arrived quickly and was of great support as we rested and readied our birthing preparations. Once it was safer to have this baby on the outside than to stay put on the inside, our doula reminded us of all the natural stimulations to begin contractions. Raspberry tea, massages on the big rolling ball, and Ken's favorite, nipple stimulation. Ken made for a great coach and was gentle and supportive. He kept the door to our room private, which entailed playing bouncer at our door to limit visits from friends and family who were not supposed to be a part of our birth plan.

Amazingly, something worked because my contractions began. My doctor was also a friend who had come to my side in preparation of delivering this baby that night. The time was now. My doula reminded me to breathe through a chant I had learned at her side to calm the energy. Unbelievably, I'd arrived at nine centimeters dilated without much pain. I was called brave by our doctor. Then she checked in on our baby and realized the oxygen levels were dangerously low, so I'd have to receive some medical support. Although I desperately dreamt of a natural childbirth, I dreamt more of a baby, so I agreed to do whatever it took. In moments I was receiving a steady drip of pitocin. Then I felt the world. Bravery was thrown out the window. This drug caused me to have an out-of-body experience.

I turned to Ken, and he reminded me to breathe. "This is the part where you exhale," he reminded me. It took hours, and that team hung tough. At one point, I said I was done and didn't want to do this anymore. The doctor and Ken smiled but had to seriously remind me that that wasn't an option. The nerve. Then I pleaded. Please don't judge me, but I implored. I wanted drugs, and I wanted them now! This time laughing, our doctor calmly reminded me that no one was judging. It was simply too late to receive that sort of assistance. She knew I did not want to be wheeled away for a C-section, so she attempted one last coaching tactic. She spoke of a ring of fire and said to push through that. Yup, that was exactly the descriptor that guided me into bringing our oldest into this world.

It was a boy! They laid his scraggly 4.6-pound, 18-inch-long body across my bare chest before whisking him off to his new NICU home. He could breathe on his own, thanks to all the answered prayers and getting both doses of the steroids in him. We had more work to do, because for some reason we had agreed on a girl's name, but the now known boy's name still needed his middle name.

The days that came felt more like checking into work than becoming his mother. It would take this new job for me to get to know my now baby boy all over again. As if I had gone to get my hair done, I checked myself out to attend a friend's dinner gathering. I had a confession of just how far removed I was from my new calling. Upon returning, the hospital gave a stern warning of their care for me and baby, requiring me to remain in place. From womb to crib at home would take nearly three weeks in the NICU.

Because I'd never changed a diaper prior to then, I enjoyed every lesson those NICU nurses provided. As an only child, Ken and I were on par for diaper duties. And because our son required a feeding tube, both Ken and I could partake in some of the feedings once he graduated to a bottle. A whole new meaning to motherhood took place when we transferred from the terrible, hospital-grade pump to nursing. He still depended on the bottle but grew to nurse more than not. That created a new bond, one that quickly left me unable to separate from him, unlike just a few days earlier. As I watched the activity that surrounded his plastic warming home, other babies came and went through these secure doors. One baby left with an aunt because his mom would not return. This aunt made it her job to attempt to soothe any of her nephew's new world side effects. The baby girls who came through thrived quicker than the boys. And so with each passing day, especially the days that followed at home with our new bundle of joy, were just that, joy-filled.

Ken wore our son like a pendant on his chest for naps. I carried him so easily with his handful of pounds. And I learned to be his protector from the outside world because he could so easily develop infections that other full-term babies wouldn't be as vulnerable to. What he lacked in stature, he made up for in his bright-eyed, serious stares of his new world. As it became safe to do so, we would take botanical garden strolls and lunch dates at True Foods in the Biltmore together. We had become inseparable—until I was asked to return to work. That was when I realized how much of a momma bear I had become. To even consider the idea of separation from my caring completely for him was like asking me to return to some cooped-up jail. I loved my job, but I loved this new being more. However, given our recent real estate hardships, we had no other option but to have me return. My only consolation was that between my mother and a sweet friend who ran her digital business from home, they would care for him while I worked. And so began my grappling for my newfound purpose in life: mommyhood.

Later that spring, closer to our son's original due date, I was driving down Lincoln Road, or Paradise Valley's church row, one of my favorite hillside roads to take. I was listening to a live national talk from Pastor Charles Swindoll, whom

I'd lovingly come to know later as Paw Paw Chuck as we read his devotional stories to our boys. That day he spoke to the heart of following God. On this Good Friday, he asked who might still not have asked their heavenly Father for an eternal home. I'd heard the ask before. I considered myself a believer, but I had never taken that ask for myself. I'll be honest in that I felt as though I had no choice but to pull that car over and follow along to his every word. I bowed my head and gave my life to Jesus over those airwaves with someone I'd never met, yet it was more real and convicting than any of my past encounters. In that moment in afternoon traffic, I had just done the very thing that I had never really considered: give my life over to a very real and holy God. Jesus and I were officially an item.

I drove myself to our church's Good Friday service and asked Ken to join me. From this Good Friday on, it would become my most favorite service of all. If you've ever attended one, there's little hope to gather as lights grow dim during the service until you're left in the dark. You then exit the doors and wait for the hope that rises on Sunday with its Easter celebrations. But I know how the whole story goes. I know this Good Friday, our good Father gave it all for us. His one and only Son would obey to the point of death so we can have this eternal home with Him, forever. And this was now my truth, a forever home I could claim out of nothing I did and everything He did for me. I would have made this a general message for others and not claimed it before this moment. This was now a real response for me.

In my gleeful state of having just made this declaration, I did have some misguided expectations. I assumed much would come to be taken care of. Whether it was our finances or for me to be able to be a stay-at-home mom. Therefore when no changes came, when greater financial disarray came our way and some of the hardest marital times were had, I half expected to leave this Jesus choice. The irony is it never crossed my mind. Times got tougher, but He wasn't to blame. He was a strange comfort like a friend journeyed alongside me. And as we lost property and budgets got tighter, we remained committed to our newfound family, home, and faith. Whatever was left would be enough, because having Jesus was enough.

> Behold, I have inscribed you on the palm of my hands. (Isaiah 49:16 NASB)

His Presence

Spring 2010

Now home with a son, and balancing any time away from home, I would often find myself weeping to our brief separation. I wanted to be the one witnessing it all. Instead, I would witness much of it through hearsay by mom or my friend, our son's main caregivers. It didn't hurt that this friend was and still is an accomplished photographer. Her creative poses of our bundle of joy always made this momma's heart soar. The best moment was when she and her hubby had discovered our baby's favorite artist, Barry White, particularly "Can't Get Enough of Your Love." That one afternoon in a bout of our son's fussiness, they decided to let random songs play in an attempt to calm him in the small bouncy seat that was placed near their reach. Then they heard it. Or rather, they noticed the lack of hearing him. Curious, they turned down the song. The vocals returned more upset than before at our son's protest of this song being gone. Surely enough, when they turned it back up, our baby couldn't get enough of Barry White's soothing love song.

We questioned their discovery, so they copied the song on CD and challenged us to give it a go while en route to visit family out west. At one point, our son began his loud cry, so we popped in Barry's "Can't Get Enough of Your Love," and silence ensued behind us. It was true. Volume to the song down; volume of our son's protest up. Whatever the fuss may have been, we kept the song on loop for the last hour of that ride. Sad to say, Ken and I did get enough of that love song.

These moments made me realize just how very involved I still was in our baby's world—and that I too could experience these firsts. Yet I still struggled with the balance of work and home life. One thing that stopped were any of the long afterhours I used to pull. As soon as five o'clock hit, I ran out the door to our little abode, where I would relieve my mom from her grandmotherly duties, though it was not hard for her to dote on him and us. To be honest, Mom was running our home in more than one way. By the time I arrived home, laundry was done and put away. Dinner was ready and baby was fed, singing along to the tunes of *Ni Hao, Kai-Lan* for those Nick Jr. fans. My mom still claims our son's prodigy Greek skills in naming her grandmother's nickname, Momma Yeye. Ken and I quickly realized it was the association of that animated series' main character's grandfather, Ye-ye, with his mom's mom.

It was a great ease to come home to all taken care of. So why the wrestling? I'm not sure whether it was pride or some wrong expectations I had, but in my dreams of mothering, I was a homemaker too. Momma Yeye meant no harm, but as we exchanged household duties before she left each night, I thought it more like taking over her duties and felt a bit of a stranger in my own home. This lie would be tackled years later with a cross-country move, but in that moment I wanted more. I wanted the whole job and realized no job could satisfy this desire. What I didn't see was that nothing could satisfy me but my desire to get alone and get with God.

So on that day, when Momma Yeye called to say that Dad and I would have to read to her possible cancer results once received, I thought the worst—not that she would have cancer, but that I didn't want to be the support or caregiver she needed. The worst was realized, both in her having confirmed stage three breast cancer and in my not being there as she needed me. I blamed my being a young mother on most of it, but truly it was my inability to serve her after years of struggling in our relationship. My selfishness surfaced as I ran the other way and occupied myself with our home and baby's needs. Sweet friends and a community would gather around Mom, but not her one and only kid.

On the day Dad and I were to give her the positive cancer results, it was after our church service. We had a prayer time at the altar, where she requested us all go. There, she looked at us and shared her already knowing of her having cancer. Dad and I looked at each other to see who had let it out, but she reassured us that she realized the results would not win in the end. She and God had this. And as skeptical as I was given her past tendencies to literally faint when overwhelmed, I saw God come alive in my mother's cancer. She ate more salmon and kale than ever before, prayed often, and even brought empanadas to her oncologist and nurses. Then when I finally braved going to one of her chemotherapy sessions, I found people of all ages bundled under blankets to receive their dosing. She vibrantly held meetings on her phone, spoke to fellow peers. and often laughed with anyone who would listen. She was a joy to be around. I knew then that it was Jesus in my mom whom I was getting to meet.

She would later share in her own story to thousands regarding how God met her in the middle of her own questioning. The pool's water fountain that gushed at her questioning, "If you're real, Lord, then show Yourself," in the middle of the night outside as she prayed. Her sitting at a friend's table and seeing the Bible rest with a highlighted verse, Isaiah 41:10 (NIV), "So do not fear, for I am with you." Her seeing figures that came to show up as Jesus with two of His apostles standing near her, unable to open her eyes during any of the radiation treatments. Her finding out a month after her own diagnosis that her only sister also had the same cancer in the same area—and how their sisterhood strengthened until the day my aunt passed away. Both reconciled and forgave any past hurts, which were many given their own hardships with a mother who had been physically and emotionally abusive. My mom seeking to reconcile with all, even me, truly showed me the goodness of God. One afternoon, after having her over for some more salmon and kale, she turned to me and apologized. "For the thousands of wrongs I've done to you, please forgive me." I never thought I'd meet my mother like this. She was accountable. And in that moment, I was amazed to see the powerful presence of God at work in her. I too asked forgiveness, though it would take me much longer. Our relationship reconciled in such a way that I didn't think possible on this side of heaven. That's the ministry of reconciliation we are called to.

> Therefore, if anyone is in Christ, the new creation has come: The old has gone, the new is here! All this is from God, who reconciled us to himself through Christ and gave us the ministry of reconciliation: that God was reconciling the world to himself in Christ, not counting people's sins against them. And he has committed to us the message of reconciliation. (2 Corinthians 5:17–19 NIV)

Our Prayer

Winter 2010

After visiting Ken's family on the East Coast, we boarded the flight back home on New Year's Eve night, with our son fighting a low-grade fever. We did not think much of it given his tendencies for ear infections, and we took our seats. They started showing the movie *Eat, Pray, Love*, which felt like a bit of an escape as our son nodded off, but we were jarred back into our own movielike existence. Our son awoke and became as stiff as a board as he straightened and began to seize. His eyes rolling back and his mouth foamed. I impulsively asked for a doctor on the flight. I must've hollered it half a dozen times before the woman across the aisle asked to take my place. A firefighter switched seats with me as I helplessly watched her take over and place our son's now limp body across her lap. By then the flight attendants and an EMT from the front of the plane had made their way over to the scene. She requested oxygen to be brought over, and I looked for help in Ken's eyes. He simply mouthed, "Just pray."

I turned away from the scene, and this firefighter's companion and the surrounding passers-by met my gaze and asked if they could pray with me. Their request stunned me. "To whom?" they asked. I quickly mumbled Jesus. They took over. Their words held us all up as we began to cry at the thought of the unknown and this awful image of our son seemingly slipping away. I can't recall all their sweet words as they fervently prayed. I simply remember a few moments later being brought back to the scene at hand with relief. The oxygen was helping him breathe. His sideways position had to remain to avoid suffocation, and the crew had the pilot communicating with the closest control tower over a possible emergency landing for care. The midway stop we were already bound for was Denver, Colorado, before our final destination to Phoenix. It just so happened to have a children's hospital. Denver's airport physician, also in communication with our pilot, received our son's report and urged us to continue the flight there because they'd be prepared and able to handle our family's needs.

It was all so much, and after I excused myself for a restroom break, I prayed alone. In that small space, I had enough room to be completely undone. In my plea with God, I begged him to do anything to spare our son and allow Ken and me to remain his earthly parents for years to come. I offered to do anything humanly possible to save him. As I looked up with tearful eyes, I heard, "Write." Write? Had I really heard right? Write about this? I agreed, half unknowingly of what it meant or would entail. And as I returned to our seat, we received even greater relief.

My son was at stable levels, and the firefighter and EMT shared their professional view that this was an episode of febrile seizures. Ken and I were unaware of what it meant, but trusted that it meant recoverable. The plane landed, and we gave our thanks to those heroes as we were let off first and ahead of the gate's entrance. They had brought a ladder to usher us directly into an ambulance for the children's hospital. The way that vehicle maneuvered past the runway and onto the icy roads of Denver only elevated our already heightened state. Not to mention, our baggage continued the trip home as we took this detour.

The children's hospital didn't take any risks and immediately admitted us for the night. Unfortunately, upon admission, our son began this haunting episode all over again. He would go on to have three seizures in total over a twenty-four-hour period. He had now been diagnosed with complex febrile seizures. Due to this, further testing with another night's stay would occur. They'd have to rule out meningitis and the like with a spinal tap that was unbearable to observe in its preparations, let alone allow the invasiveness. Unable to make anything simple out of this New Year we had just entered, we began to alert our loved ones.

After we told our families and friends of the detour and son's state, they immediately began to pray and assist. They picked up our items back home. My boss, living just twenty minutes outside of Denver, brought us the most humbling love package we could dream of, filled with clothes for Ken and me and even a Curious George stuffy and book for our son. It was this sort of outpouring that gave us true comfort in the waiting. All the results came back negative. As for these complex seizures that came on with a high spike fever, well, they were simply the body's way of protecting itself. Though they were horrific to witness, a dose of acetaminophen and ibuprofen contained greater side effects. Our son's probability of outgrowing them after age five was high, and the likelihood of a continued seizure disorder only increased by a small percent in comparison to the rest of the population. In other words, he was going to be fine. The hospital discharged us with two donated blankets made by hospital volunteers and an unbelievably reduced-price car seat given ours had returned home with the luggage. Denver Children's would forever hold a special place in our hearts.

Given our uncertainty in it all, we decided to take the rest of the day to check into the nearest hotel and attempt a proper night's rest. We wanted to get showered and rest in a proper bed for the night. Knowing the next available flight awaited the following day wasn't exactly our most comforting thought. Both Ken and I struggled with the idea of reliving this recent memory. We would have to put our trust in knowing that if we ever witnessed an episode again, the truth was it was not hurtful to him. If anything, it was life-preserving. Though not immediately, he did go on to have a few more episodes until age five. It was amazing to hear of how many friends and even family members had known of or undergone these same episodes as a child. This brought us all great comfort, but it was in seeing our good God at work in and around us that gave us the greatest of comforts, knowing that He is a God who comforts best when we are in pain.

> Praise be to the God and Father of our Lord Jesus Christ, the Father of compassion and the God of all comfort, who comforts us in all our troubles, so that we can comfort those in any trouble with the comfort we ourselves receive from God. (2 Corinthians 1:3 NIV)

Our Move

Winter 2011

My first grown-up move was cross-country with a toddler in tote. We made northern Virginia, Ken's old stomping grounds, our new home. As much as I had romanticized this move, I would quickly realize that my homesickness ran deep. A longing for our former home and proximity to my parents would have me unable to settle. Marrying at twenty-two would have its impact on me now. Ken had already witnessed some of this prior to our move, when I vacationed without him on the Mayan Riviera. This time, it would have a longer-lasting impact on us both. Having never moved away or even moved out until I was married left me unsure of myself in all of my roles, whether as a wife, a mother, or at work. This insecurity fostered often when I attempted to move out of my parents' place during Ken's and my engagement, only to have my mother move her offices into my two-bedroom rental they were helping me pay for. And most nights, she would crash at my place, so really it was more like *The Golden Girls* gone wrong.

This new move was necessary not just for Ken's work but my overall detachment and reattachment to complete adulthood. I was conditioned to have Mom's help. Though we had just relocated next to Ken's family, where my brother-in-law's sweet wife visited this future residence and neighborhood on our behalf, their policy was definitely not Latin. They'd wait to be invited. It was what I thought I had wanted all along. And though I had an overlap of a few weeks without employment, I thought I'd be able to relish in full-time mommyhood. Instead, I often broke down not just due to our new routines and homecare but in establishing our new network, be it friends, church, the grocer, or medical care. The first morning in our new place, before Ken left for work, I asked to visit the local Trader Joe's. These were the days prior to our smartphone map devices, so I had written out directions. Well, this new mixing bowl area of traffic mixed me up. And in an instant, not only had I missed my stop, but I was well on my way into the city. With the monument in front of me upon entering our nation's capital and no understanding of these clover-like systems to return home, this would not be a warm introduction to our relocation.

After finally returning home at Ken's guidance on my flip phone, I tried to settle in with no groceries and our toddler's play needs. Once Ken left for work and our son began his nap, I tried to get quiet, but I was anxious over this new place and its winding roads. I knew I needed to talk to someone. With Ken's family working and friends out west still sleeping, I turned to prayer. It was not usually my first option; I often thought of it as if it was a last hope. I needed to be heard. God knew how what I needed most was to listen. And how He captured my attention, I'll not forget. While I was cross-legged on our basement carpet and gazing outward into our forested backyard, I began to breathe. I rested my eyes on the prayer Bible my sweet girlfriend had equipped me with from our past church, and I read through a random devotion alongside the scriptures. In an instant I saw it. Like a speck in my eye, something bright moved my attention up and out. It was the state's feathered friend. This red cardinal was striking to the late fall background. It flew toward the ground to take its morning hops in front of our sliding back door. I wondered whether it could sense my presence. As soon as I thought about it, this cardinal hopped closer toward me. There in front of me, I knew that God had become so real again. Though not in the shape of a hummingbird, it was still a bird, and it called me closer to him. It was God asking me to trust him, knowing that if He clothes and cares for even these, how much more will He do for us, for me.

I'd like to admit that was the end of any of my sadness. The reality was that for weeks, even after securing my new telework position and right childcare fit for our toddler, I turned to what I thought would grant me the greatest comfort: people. And many friends did, old and new alike. Many phone calls out west would help me smile and laugh at our times spent together. New neighbors added as Facebook friends would see my posts seeking home out west again and invite me over for tea. These new meetings slowly became close friendships where our kids could play, and we made so many new memories in our annual gatherings for any holiday or reason we could find to get together. But I knew something had to change that they could not do for me. My outlook remained foggy until the day I was able to find the true reason for my Eeyore outlook.

While helping to promote for work a Spanish-resource on depression, I was tasked to read it thoroughly before sharing it with future clients. By having to read this, I got lost in checking all the boxes for myself. After talking with a friend out west, I burst out that I had depression. She responded with a sigh of relief, telling me that I had to come to it on my own terms. It was such a strange step, that of awareness. It absolutely became the first step in my seeking professional help out east. I knew that I had anxious tendencies, but depression had its own set of criteria. Anxiety had me insecure or timid in my ventures, but depression had me removed from venturing at all. Anxiety gave me hesitation, whereas depression was a lack of desire to do most anything at all. It would take several referrals to both Christian and non-Christian counselors before settling on a female Muslim therapist whom I connected to the most. Her ability to listen and give insight and a dose of reality with conviction for change would remain a faithful and helpful relationship for years. And her openness and respect to hear of my Christian walk and application to life made for a greater trust. But later on, even this would be challenged not for its help but for the crisis that would require theology to be married with this profession for complete healing.

> And whatsoever ye do, do it heartily, as unto the Lord, and not unto men. (Colossians 3:23 KJV)

Our Loss

Fall 2012

A year into this cross-country move, we were pregnant again! My waistline immediately knew to expand right back to its enlarged self. When at the providers for my annual blood work, I urged for a pregnancy test too. The results were positive. I was certain this would elate Ken because we were about to celebrate his birthday with extended family at home. When I did share, we were thrilled. As the youngest of three, he certainly had more to say in the world of siblings than I did. Knowing my folks were unable to have another child, I was aware of this being a privilege. We relished and shared early on with our whole family. That quickly turned into friends who are like family, including a sweet family friend and "other mother" to me, also from Argentina. She was my dance therapist, Pilates trainer, and overall confidant. Her congratulatory call that week came as no surprise.

When the spotting began, though we were familiar with this happening with our oldest, it was still unnerving. When it didn't stop and only worsened, I recall the sweetness of my sister-in-law and nurse as she urged me to rest after having been in her home when symptoms progressed. She knew then what we would come to confirm later with our doctors: a complete miscarriage had occurred. We had so much hope that this two-month-old child was still with us as they searched the monitors for a heartbeat. The silence left us to begin the days of mourning ahead.

How could so much joy turn into this loss within moments? Family tried desperately to comfort us—Mom with her own experiences of multiple miscarriages, and others with their presence and meals. Because I had a scheduled work trip up north, we thought it best I continue as planned to help take my thoughts off it all. As I packed, my other mother and former dance therapist called on the phone. I gladly took her call to hear her comforting me. Knowing me so intimately, she reassured me that God had another plan and said that though this sweet angel was with Him now, He would bring along another child. I thanked her, but I wanted this child, not another. It was still comforting to hear her voice so real and alive.

The next day, I headed north and tried to leave behind what I could. It was a quick three-day training. On that last day, it began to snow. I was still rather new to the extreme climate changes in the seasons, so I embraced its covering all around us. Strangely enough, I began to think about my other mother, who had called prior to my trip. I was reminded of the time she had taken me skiing with her and her boys. They were so adventurous as a family, and I had never skied. She made sure that I could graduate from the bunny slope to the blue course before we settled in for the night with hot chocolate and movies. With a smile, I brought my thoughts back to our wrap-up session before heading out.

On the way to the airport, Ken called. Strangely enough, it was about my friend I think of as my other mother. I was uncertain why he was calling me about her, but he then revealed the unthinkable. She had been killed. He had to repeat it for me, and I was blinded by the statement. The others in the car began to redirect their attention to me as we carpooled to the airport. Ken went on to say that her life was taken at the hand of her husband and witnessed by her youngest son, then a young adult. I became numb, lost all sense of my whereabouts, and wanted to board a flight directly back to that home where I had seen her last. Back to Phoenix.

It was before Thanksgiving, and as the world prepared for festive gatherings, we prepared for the loss of these two souls. Their children had become orphaned overnight. All I could do was question on the flight back west, “How can any comfort come from this senseless act?” Instead of looking further inward, I moved my eyes onto the scriptures in search of hope. One stood out, enough for me to write it down for them and enclose it in personalized copies of an Oswald Chambers devotional, *My Utmost for His Highest*. Whether this would ever give them any comfort was not up to me. It was simply my need to obey the nudge of sharing it. And so I did, along with the request to perform a tango in her honor as asked by her sister. Unsure of it all, I obeyed that call too. After all the years of training in her studio alongside other students, it was a way to honor and be a part of her legacy. The one who made it her profession to be a comfort to others had left us seeking our own.

In my attempt to muster through the holidays for our son amid the tragedies, I was confronted by those I loved most to move on and to return. There was no comfort to be found in anyone or anything but Jesus. I rocked myself alone, chanting for Jesus to come into that space until I could calm down long enough to attempt to reason with myself. To somehow snap out of this dazed and confused state. I decided to put on a sort of show. To no longer show emotion over these real losses but to hide it away so as to go on with it all. One could say I was functioning, at least for a while, until I could no longer mask my coming undone.

For I am convinced that neither death nor life, neither angels nor demons, neither the present nor the future, nor any powers, neither height nor depth, nor anything else in all creation, will be able to separate us from the love of God that is in Christ Jesus our Lord. (Romans 8:38–39 NIV)

Our Hope

Spring 2013

Perpetual sickness. Nothing to show for it. No pregnancy. No real reason for these pains. Yet they were very real. And bloody, in fact. Regardless of what I ate, the bleeding and cramping was outside of the menstrual cycle. One endoscopy and colonoscopy later, the GI doctor redirected me: "You need another kind of physician." He shared how stress can lead to these symptoms. These very real outward signs were a sign for me to get help from a professional who could handle the very deep depression I could not shake off. I was not unfamiliar with seeking this sort of help given my recent bout with our East Coast move. I sparked up my professional help counsel again and came across something very different.

Given Ken's work at what would eventually become our home church, he wasn't as comfortable worshipping there at the time because his client would often but kindly ask about the project's status. Therefore we turned to another just as sound and strong church. An Anglican one. We had not heard about this branch of Christianity, but we came to find out its historical roots were deep. We connected quickly with a local group of families that would meet outside the church to have the kids play while the adults had Bible study and discussion. We grew close to these families. While we did much and grew greatly under its guidance, we remained open to options closer to home. It wasn't always the easiest to pack us up early on Sunday for a thirty-minute drive one way. After having come from a Methodist church out west, we remained open to visiting many of them near home. Though we wouldn't continue visiting one in particular as a family, I would go myself, though not for Sunday service.

I had read of the local Methodist church offering a program on losing loved ones, called GriefShare®. These classes would be held weekly for a couple of months by one of their pastors and counselors. This program and the pastor would become my lifeline to tasting life's goodness again. Nearly nine months after the loss of my friend and our miscarriage, I was back to what I believed to be normal—normal in that I did all the normal demands of the day, be it changing sheets or hosting a meeting. As I sat down in the trailer adjacent to the church's main building, I met with this pastor and another one or two members who were in their own grief over a recent loss of a loved one. Unsure of what it would all be able to really do, I committed to showing up and completing the weekly homework. Videos would play at the beginning of each week by co hosts, a couple who had mourned the loss of more than one child. To see them both able to share in this grief resource was enough hope for me to continue sitting in the awkward pain of my reality. Soon the class became a safe house. The homework was a sort of continued connection to that safety where I could let it all be known and feel known.

Summer 2013

By the end of the GriefShare program, I had gained so much insight into grief, past just the stages and seeing all the in between, like the void in the roles that those loved ones left. I could release and finally grieve honestly. And in that honest space, I was able to receive His lightness and allow my God to shoulder the burden. Therefore when a friend in our church family group asked me to join in the women's retreat and room with her, I was ready to go. The conference speaker, Ellen Vaughn, would bring us all so much joy and sincere laughter in sharing her then recent publication of *Come, Sit, Stay*, which I brought home and obeyed every call. But my gift came in the most unlikely form. Over the weekend, before the next scheduled meeting, my friend and roommate was intuitive enough to ask how I really was doing. She sensed I'd healed much but not yet been given what God was wanting for me. She asked if it were OK to lead me in a sort of visual prayer time. Not expecting much, I accepted.

With eyes closed, she prayed aloud, though of what I still cannot recall. I simply know that at some point, her voice was no longer at the forefront, but a clear picture in my mind had replaced all my surroundings. It was an open field full of flowering yellow beauties. The day was warm as the sun showed off. Walking toward me was a figure. At the same time, I was unable to look to my left, but I felt a greater warmth with a blinding light. I kept my eyes fixated on the approaching figure. Then standing in front of me was my sweet friend whom I had mourned all these long days. She was before me but not alone. Embraced in her arms was my lost child. I knew it. The baby we would not meet on this side of heaven was being presented to me in this virtual world of a vision. The love and joy on my friend's beautiful face in this vision before me is ingrained in every part of my bones. Still yearning to hold the child, I was washed in peace, and I knew that the peace that surpasses this world's understanding was the very one standing beside me. It was Jesus at my side. Though unable to see now, one day I would be shown in all His glory when we put our faith in Him. I can now imagine.

Fall 2013

I'd go on to imagine even more for our future. At the help of this Anglican church, there were prayer healing sessions referred to as Theophostic counseling. After having completed my GriefShare and wanting to move into a renewed time of prayer, I opened myself up to this new way of counseling. I made my appointment for after Ken's workday and was greeted by two of the church's members trained in this method. What occurred next still amazes me. After quick introductions, they went straight into a time of prayer, and we would remain there for the entirety of the hour. I was asked to let the Holy Spirit bring up any past or present hurts. At first it was silent. As they sat in the silence, so did I, allowing my discomfort to turn into surrender so I could hear whatever was laid on my heart. That's when memories of even our wedding day returned—more so the lack of my obeying God's nudges that left me having pleased all wedding participants, leaving the bride's requests to the side. As I shared this memory that sounded so petty, the women in the counseling room asked me to now counter that lie with the truth from what the Spirit would reveal. I was to remain silent until His prompting was made. And it was. I knew it was from Him because I would have not had this thought on my own. In that moment, I heard forgiveness and mercy. Forgiveness for losing sight of the commitment between God, Ken, and me. It was not just a marriage with my earthly man but that with my heavenly Father. He once again forgave and wanted to take it further. That one day, I would have the opportunity to renew our vows and have so much more to celebrate. This was just one of the many truths I was able to hear in response to the countless lies that were exposed that night in my session. When I was asked to end our prayer counseling session, I was given pages of these two faithful servants' notes. They had documented all the lies that I had voiced aloud and the responses I also shared aloud that the Holy Spirit imparted as His truth. I was so grateful but exhausted. On my drive home, I pulled over to relieve some of my physical sickness from such an emotional response.

Though these alternative guided healing steps did heal, I was still fighting the fog, this looming anger that my friend's painful death could have been avoided had she opened up to me, had I only known. I was retreating into an unspoken anger over her loss. I knew I was given a comfort of seeing her in heaven with our unborn child, so why the struggle yet again? I realized we were approaching the anniversary of her death, so Ken took our son to his daycare and left me at home with my thoughts. I recalled my current therapist's advice to revisit all of the items left behind in my possession by the one who left them, so I sat there. The therapist also suggested a sort of rope to pull back from the emotions, and mine was to pick up our son from his daycare. Until then, I sat with the pictures, the videos of our dance performances, the artwork we had done together, and all of the memories. I expected tears. What came was anger. Anger for her not doing more to exit the danger. Anger for all the pieces missing in an unsolvable puzzle. Knowing my time was up, I gathered myself and her things and set it aside for another day. As I left our townhouse, I tripped on a package at the front door. Not knowing when it had arrived, I quickly opened the contents to discover a book entitled *Forgiveness* by Matthew West. The package was from our local Christian station, WGTS 91.9 FM. Thinking it a thoughtful gift, I also set this aside, dismissing it as irrelevant to me.

When I awoke the next morning in a deeper fog, and to Ken's concern, I remained home to once again face the unknown and tiring battle of depression. Before leaving, Ken left me with the little book on forgiveness that had arrived the night prior. Again, I did not see its relevance, but not wanting to remain where I was, I opened and read it. The very first chapter dealt with a mother's loss of her child by a drunk driver. That was not the end of the story. The author and artist of this book released a song entitled "Forgiveness" about this mother's story. Instead of allowing the one who took her child's life to remain incarcerated, she visited him. She forgave him. They went on to foster a friendship that would end in her petitioning early release, which was granted to him. When she didn't know where to take her story, she took it to God, who took her to forgiveness. At that moment, I dropped the book and picked up pen and paper. I began to write and did not stop for several handwritten pages later. I wrote out my anger of the senseless loss and all involved. Then I wrote out of forgiveness, both in seeking it and sharing it. When I finished that last forgiveness statement and set it all down, I left it all there at the foot of the cross, never to pick it up again. I was lighter than ever before. The answer to my anger had been forgiveness, a response I could not have thought of, so my good Father did it for me.

> And the peace of God, which transcends all understanding, will guard your hearts and minds in Christ Jesus. (Philippians 4:7 NIV)

Our Truth

Winter 2014

It was no longer a harsh winter as we were once again pregnant, awaiting the birth of our second son. I was considered high risk given a history of our son's premature birth and the miscarriage that followed equated to visit not only our regular obstetrician's office but that of the high-risk doctors too. These doctors would kick in after mid pregnancy and start doing their more regular testing, including images of our baby boy. This way we were able to know the sex much earlier. We were also more than OK with not having any surprises this go around. However, to ensure the full-term of this pregnancy, they would begin to pump me with added progesterone because studies proved this method helped hold babies intact for longer. At this point, I would do just about anything to give our son a sibling.

During this time, with Ken's work of our now home church being completed, we began to worship there again. Our head pastor shared a challenge: if we had not yet done so, we should consider reading the Bible in a year. I had not, so I took him up on the challenge. Not knowing for how long this baby would stay in utero but simply grateful for the time we did have together, I decided to read aloud to him. Whatever scriptures I was doing that day in the Old Testament, Psalms and Proverbs, or New Testament would be shared with our baby as ritually as the moms who played Mozart through headphones on their growing bellies.

I often made voices for the different characters, and I enjoyed our time in these historical pages come to life and how they came to life. It was better than most dramas with all the scandal and bloodshed. I yearned for this time and our readings. It connected me to this growing baby boy inside, knowing I was speaking words over him that his Creator said. It gave me a real peace in the uncertainty of our future, a trust that there was a good plan. Therefore it was of no surprise that on one Sunday morning's sermon, when we learned about a character in particular, I was convicted this would become his name. Ken wasn't as convinced, but when I discovered the meaning behind Joseph—that God will provide a second son—you betcha it at least became his middle name. And how it suited him not only for being the younger brother but also for the joy he brought into our lives at his birth. Within moments of being placed into our arms, his mouth opened into a smile. Ken and I looked at each other and laughed out of joy. This bundle of joy has kept doing this all of his days.

It would not be until later that fall, when my folks came for a holiday visit, that I'd find myself in a pool of my tears, unable to care for our then five-month-old son. My father found me upstairs completely helpless. His asking if I was OK brought me into a sob of confessing that I was not. Mom would step in to comfort and relieve me of our baby's care so I could rest. Sleep was a true lifeline. When I lacked it, my thoughts would run even wilder. I would become a very different person after a full night's rest. Even so, I knew now that it was time to return to counseling. And so with this more tearful state, I began to meet weekly with my counselor, who would reassure me of the positive signs in such a negative state of mind. That alone brought on more shame. How could

I be feeling this way when I clearly felt such joy for this answer to prayer? Her insights would become a true comfort. Many mothers struggle with irrational thoughts while hormones regulate. Sleep, or rather the lack of it, would heighten this state. If I were to continue nursing him, this too would keep my hormones out of balance up until a year after we weaned him. My work was to continue voicing my thoughts.

The overwhelming thoughts of insecurity at any time, especially the nighttime feedings, when I thought that our baby would just fall out of my arms over our stair's banister, meant I had to say them aloud to remove their power. It's when we don't share that those thoughts become a threat or danger. How backward, I thought. I felt monstrous but followed her advice: to share and to not trust my thoughts. In her professional counsel, she reminded me that our thoughts are not our own, and it is up to us to decide which ones we'll listen to. She may not have realized the spiritual impact that had on my life. It removed so much of the guilt and shame that stirred within. These words would replay for the rest of my days to make an active choice. To choose to hear truth, both in scripture and through Christian music. When I was too tired to read, the praise music that came through the airwaves would speak truth into those early dark hours. I found the days ahead had restored peace and rest.

> This is the day which the LORD has made;
> let's rejoice and be glad in it. (Psalm 118:24 NASB)

Our Break

Spring 2015

I still wanted nothing more than to be a stay-at-home mom. Although I was grateful to telework, there were still days of commuting into the client's office. With the traffic from northern Virginia into the Maryland border, it was enough to keep me sitting for over an hour if poorly timed. I was grateful for my friend who signed up to give the full-time care both my nine-month-old and kindergartner were in need of while I refocused on work. For the most part, this worked out for us both so that she could tote her kids along or take mine to drop off her oldest at school. When one of her kiddos fell ill, I would need backup. Because our local family worked, I was often sent into a frantic scavenger for childcare. These days were rough and a sore reminder of what I would have preferred to be doing all along. Though I loved my work and received many accolades, it was the thankless work at home I desired the most.

One day, I had made other childcare plans. The plan was to be home before this sitter started her next shift. She was doing us the favor to be our backup so long as her main work could still be met. Therefore when this meeting across state lines ran long, I found myself on one of those 495-jammed lanes inching home well after when I needed to be back. With no neighbor or family available to step in at the last minute,

I began to feel a sense of panic. Ken worked a bit closer than where I was stuck but was not close enough to relieve our relief care. In the middle of the chaos, my legs began to do their old familiar trembles. While completely stopped in traffic, I sent an SOS text to a group of friends from our lifegroup at church. My plea was desperate, asking for them to pray for our need of care fast so that both my infant and five-year old would be safe. That was when these angels got to work. One of the ladies took it upon herself to turn around, cancel her hair appointment, and came to our aid. I was shocked. How could this friend be so selfless to see this struggling mom's heart and answer this above-and-beyond call? Just then, I welled up with a lot of anger—certainly not at her, but at our circumstances. The traffic. Ken's inability to come to the rescue. The work meeting that went too late. The fact that I had to still do this work, often with last-minute travel that conflicted with Ken's travels, leaving us with limited options for who could provide overnight care. It was all becoming too much.

Though I felt relief in my friend's sacrifice for our family, I proceeded to have a full-blown anxiety attack in those jammed middle lanes. It washed over me from my extremities first. I was not able to grip the steering wheel any longer because my fingers clamped together like a severe case of arthritis, so I used my elbows to blink my way over to the emergency lanes. It was not a surprise that most people also in a rush to return home would not let me over. This fueled and sped up the attack as I laid into my horn to be let over. My feet began to curl, making it hard to push the gas. I finally made it across. I couldn't unlock my fingers long enough to dial a call. Using the voice automated feature, I was able to get Ken on the phone. He sounded alarmed but never made it known, reminding me to calm down. If I could lose it any further, I did so. "Don't you think I'd have calmed down if I could?" I snapped. Knowing this attack would come to pass over the next few moments, I urged him to return home until I could drive myself again. It lasted longer than past attacks, but forty-five minutes later, I would be back on my way home. While I thought good thoughts, took deep breaths, and slowed down my mind as best as I knew how, this would become just one of my breaking points.

One kind man pulled over to check on me, and I assured him this would soon pass for me. An officer came behind me next. He was unable to legally assist me in driving my vehicle off the highway, so his only offer was an ambulance to the nearest emergency room. Those visits in the past resulted in an expensive counsel of simply finding my happy place. I kindly declined. While staring through our sunroof skyward, I followed my breath in this cramped state in search of an unseen help and hope. One that would see me in this mess and be my true rescuer. I prayed. I sang to Him. I sought His face again. Jesus was more than a friend, as my body felt warmth enter from my deep breaths in every part of this broken body. It would be in those moments that ever so slowly, my limbs released their tension. Once I finally regained feeling and fingers unlocked, I made my way home. As if these friends from our church hadn't already done enough, we had a meal and flowers brought into our home that same night. I knew then why churchgoers refer to each other as the body of Christ. They had literally become my hands and feet to step into my role as mother, both to our boys and to me. Accepting this other care slowly gave me a rising guilt that was quickly squandered by their grace.

The next day, upon getting back to normal with my friend's return for childcare, I shared our debacle. She responded much differently than I had anticipated. "Well, of course," she gasped. Her point was that I had added an infant to the equation of our home and work life, but we had not changed much of anything else. Ken and I worked full time as we climbed corporate ladders, but now we had two sons to care for, along with our aging dog. We stopped and prayed. I started to see more for our family. As the days went on, I kept in prayer, asking God why these attacks were on the rise. I had several more over the next few months—six, to be exact. God was clear that I observed when they arose. They were for the most part happening on the clock while at work. Sometimes they were in the most low-stress activities, like that of preparing a meeting agenda. These were turnkeys. So why the response? I'd come to find out sooner rather than later.

One night while at a women's ministry event, I had yet another episode. A friend would carry me in prayer outside those double doors as I exited the building. That's when, as C.S. Lewis would say, God spoke like a megaphone through the pain. It was time for me to be a stay-at-home mom full time.

I couldn't possibly stay at home. Our poor financial choices had followed us from out west. We could only afford to rent because no mortgage would back us up. To top it off, Ken's and my salaries were almost identical. How could we take a 50 percent pay cut and still live in this area? Besides, there was no way Ken would buy off on this plan. But my body was speaking louder than my mind, and I had to make a change. I wanted to share this with Ken as partners, so with much trepidation, I sat down to research and create a seventeen-slide PowerPoint in defense of this new commitment. It even included a stat on how men with their wives that stay home made more money. Anything to convince him we'd be OK.

I was not prepared for his response. He chuckled at the length and formality of what I had prepared but then turned to me and said yes. Yes? Yes. "If it's a calling from God, then it's our job to obey," he added.

And so we obeyed. I'll never forget one of my client's

responses to my two weeks' notice. She shared being jealous of my getting to do what I wanted to. She was someone I'd admired for her sacrifice at work, and she wanted something different. It amazed me to think that as we make changes, it causes others to share their own desires. As much as it was a desire of my heart, it was also a definite leap of faith for Ken and me. We had to trust that the needs of these young boys would be met. We were completely relying on our God's leading, and it wasn't overnight. Several budget cuts had to be made. Certainly we could no longer afford cable. There was a lot of meal planning. But nine months later, before the new year, God met us with his provision through an unexpected promotion for Ken. To the dollar of our budgeted line items, it met all of our needs. This became our new mode of living: to pray first and then trust in God's leading. As a wise friend had shared, we had asked the Holy Spirit to establish and root us in our decision if it was his will. If it was not his will, He should remove that option entirely from our lives, making it less important to us.

> Do not merely listen to the word, and so deceive yourselves. Do what it says. (James 1:22 NIV)

Our Belief

Spring 2016

When I first moved out east, my sister-in-law made our move a reality by connecting Ken with our now church to win the work of a second-phase project that would expand its lobby and worship space. She had invited me to what the church called Breakaway, held on Tuesday mornings. I made it out only once before I entered into my then new telework position. Once we decided I'd be a full-time stay-at-home mom, and knowing Breakaway offered childcare, it was a no-brainer for me to sign us up. Our second son could enjoy a safe and loving space, and so did I. The singing as a collective group of women before breaking out into our smaller cohorts for class was a highlight. This heart prep time at the beginning, not singing, had us listening to various women's testimonies. Often stories were about their journeys with Christ. I felt so new, both in my role at home but in this Christian environment. Yet, I am one of those strange birds that actually enjoys public speaking. Though the thought of what these women did was unnerving, so exposed and so full of a conviction, I lacked.

I remember thinking and praying that one day I'd like to have a message like theirs, not realizing what I was asking. Well, this spring I'd have the opportunity to sign up for a study by Priscilla Shirer about the armor of God. In this study, we would have a video shown of Priscilla teaching before going into our study groups. One video rocked my world. She talked about Satan as a whack-a-mole game. To think of our real enemy like this was different. The thought of Satan makes me think of the cartoon cape and ears; to be honest, he didn't seem very real at all. But when Priscila went on to share, she talked about the stuff in our lives that pops up. Like the whack-a-mole game, you go to hit it, only to have something else pop up next. There were so many distractions. Now, transfer this to Satan and how he may not be very creative as he recycles our past mistakes, but he's persistent to ensure we are faced with it often. And then take it one step further. We are whacking on top of the table, but what happens when we open the curtains to look below the table of this game? What will we find pushing these moles to the surface? Satan. In that moment, at the round table in a room among more than sixty women, I saw him for the first time. I realized just how very real Satan was by disguising himself in this more unseen way.

Sadly, it didn't end there. Because Satan had me convinced of his being invisible, making him seem fictional, he also made me believe the same about God. My self-doubt rooted in not having the burning bushes, split seas, or other visible works of His left me blinded. I bought into the lie that both were fictional characters made up in my mind. I wanted so much to shout it from the mountaintop, but knowing my Achilles' heel was pride, I stayed quiet unless asked. I wanted God to call me forward and not go ahead of Him for once. What I didn't expect, besides very soon having the opportunity to share this discovery, was that I would receive an even greater revelation.

Later that week, I had another restless night. Our dog of nearly fifteen years was barely able to walk, let alone hold his restroom abilities. After cleaning yet another mess in the dark of the night, I found myself wide-eyed and led to our then townhome hallway between the kids' rooms and the shared bathroom. I opened up our study guide to a passage from the Old Testament of the Bible, 2 Kings 6. It talked about Elisha and his servant. I did not know much of his life. As I read on, I came to learn how at one point, Elisha and his servant faced a very real army in front of them. The king of Aram wanted to know why Elisha knew all about his dreamworld and shared this with the king of Israel. This king sent a strong force of horses and chariots to surround the city. Elisha's servant was very afraid. He asked in fear for what they could do. Here's where it gets good. Elisha calmed his fears with a prayer, asking the Lord to open the eyes of his servant. And what should he see but horses and chariots of fire surrounding them where they stood.

I was amazed at this very real account of a world that we can remain so blinded to, and in that moment I apologized. I got down on my knees and asked God to forgive me, to forgive my doubts of his existence. I asked for help that He too would open my eyes. And in that moment, in that very real place, something so unreal happened next. As though a robber had clobbered me, I fell on my back. It was both quick and slow as time stood still. I was lying flat on my back, but it was not of my doing. I thought I might have been influenced by one too many charismatic scenes from churches where an altar call has one fainting. I had no choice but to remain belly up on that floor. I tried so hard to open my eyes but could not. Instead, the brightest of lights came down. Warmth soothed any fears. It was so loving, so freeing, and so real, like a father showing up and giving an orphaned child an embrace. As quick as it came, it left. I opened my eyes to the beige walls and dark cool night, and the warmth was gone. And yet not. If I believed, if I had faith to know my God is a real God. He showed up in fires or with chariots back then, but He still shows up in a real way today for those who put their faith and trust in His Son.

Without being connected to the leaders at Breakaway, the women's ministry director reached out to me in hopes that I would share my testimony. She did not know any of my personal events and discoveries with God as of late, which only confirmed that He was more than watching. He wanted His truth to be known and was asking me to step up. I knew I had to share, and though I normally would jump at the option to speak in public, this was frightening. As scary as it is to type it here and make it known to you, it was just as exposing to share this truth then. The what-ifs of all that the audience could think flooded my mind. Then His truth came to mind, and I had only an audience of one. So long as He knows the truth, that was all I was expected to share. I must have timed my testimony dozens of times to get it into their five-minute requirement. Not only did I plan on sharing this testimony at the closing brunch, but I felt led to sing aloud a part of our oldest son's favorite artist's top hit at the time, "Move" by Toby Mac. I got on that stage with one slide behind me of our oldest in his self-made cardboard armor, and I told of my discovery of how real is our enemy who blinded me from a real relationship with my living God. I then proceeded to do the unthinkable: I sang. Although I admit to my strengths, I also do the same of my weaknesses. My singing is reserved for the shower or in my car with the kids. I prayed my voice would not crackle and pop.

As I walked off the stage to utter silence and no applause, I knew I had just made myself so vulnerable. Like a wave, this real enemy came to attack me with all of his might over what I had just done. That my foolish attempt to share had been just that, of a fool. But in the next day and even year, friends and strangers would slowly resurface and approach me about that moment when I shared my testimony. They talked about how it strengthened their own ability to do the same, to share just how real God had been in each of their lives.

The next year would bring so much that I will go into next. But in the midst of what I would go through, I'd find myself one day roaming the local farmers market, lost in what had just been thrown at me. After dropping off our oldest at his Lego camp, I was surprised to be addressed by a stranger. She asked if, just over a year ago, I had given a talk at Breakaway. She then thanked me for the courage to share and went on to talk about her severe depression right in the middle of this open-aired market. We would spend the next hour until camp was over sharing about how God is in the good and the bad, and how much more we come to him in the bad and how He sees us back into his goodness. This serendipity, this happenstance wasn't chance or coincidence at all. It was my very real helper coming to the rescue.

> Finally, be strong in the Lord and in the strength of His might. Put on the full armor of God, so that you will be able to stand firm against the schemes of the devil. (Ephesians 6:10–11 NASB)

Our Miracle

Winter 2017

"This is by far your best pregnancy," he told me. Thirteen years after the first, we were expecting our now third son. Later that same week, I'd be checked into a local ward for psychiatric review. How did it get so bad, so fast? Progesterone. In other words, more PMS-like hormones to keep our baby in utero for longer. Because our oldest was a preemie and we miscarried our second pregnancy, they took every precaution on this geriatric (ripe age of thirty-five) old mother. Therefore in a matter of days, I'd go from the picture of health to a sobbing mess. On one particularly cold and dark night, I'd walk out on my family tearfully, thinking they'd all be best without my presence. Within days, I'd find myself lying in tears on the floor and unable to take care of our then two-year-old. The simple task of going to the store for milk would become yet another breaking point. Instead of bringing me into the doctor's office for help, after calling her office and only speaking with the nurse as our liaison, my then obstetrician sent me to our local emergency room, feeling helpless. I had a long history of anxiety and prior postpartum after our second son, whom this same obstetrician had delivered, so my anxious tendencies were not new to our doctor. Not knowing any better, in need of being our own best advocates, we followed her suggestion of going into the emergency room for a psychiatric review given my now suicidal ideations.

A dear friend whose children were away at college took me and our second son to the local emergency room. There, I'd be ushered directly into the emergency room without any wait and met with my new assigned guardian. Their policy was to not question the symptom and treat for the worst-case scenario. And it was becoming a nightmare come true. I was unable to remain alone, so this assigned guardian would ensure my safety—or so they said. My suicidal ideations alarmed anyone I came in contact with, including the professionals. My sweet friend was even asked to usher away our son, and that was when I truly gave into my residence on this island of isolation. I can still see our son's tearful response to going home with my friend, leaving his mom behind. His walk down that hall would haunt me for the duration of my stay, and I wanted to run after him. The next hours were full of questions, evaluations, and assessments by all staff except the psychiatrist's review, which I desperately sought at the direction of my doctor. I was informed that no psychiatrist would be seeing me that day or any day. For a formal review, I'd have to be checked into their mental ward. The on-call behavioral specialist recommended this voluntary check-in. My then psychologist would be consulted and felt no other choice given my state but to agree with my doctor's over-the-phone evaluation. Realizing that no psychiatrist could make rounds on their emergency floor and half understanding what was about to happen, Ken and I agreed to this more formal and elective review in hopes of healing.

What I didn't expect were the two security guards that would then be placed at my side to escort me. They requested the removal of all personal articles, including my wedding ring. It felt as if I had just made a criminal move. In fact, it was more than a feeling—I was now naked and afraid, and not just for myself but for this little man growing inside of me, fighting to understand why his mom was sending such anxious juices his way. They ushered me up to a new floor. The ceiling seemed half its normal height. Possibly it was due to the nurses station having been enclosed by glass for their protection. But where was my protection? I asked for the only thing that came to mind. "Do you have a Bible?"

How could my Gretel-looking assigned nurse have such a sweet demeanor in such an imprisoned place? Without hesitating, she gave me a miniature New Testament Bible to keep. She also reminded me that the Gideon folk had made it there too, with the entire version found bedside. I quickly went back into my room, where doors had to remain open. Even though it was now nighttime, and the start of the weekend meant it would mean a definite overnight stay, I did what I could to settle in until I could be seen the next day for this unending wait of a psychiatric review. I opened that white, leather-bound New Testament Book that fit into the palm of my hand and flipped to the index. I thought, *What hope can you give me if I have suicidal ideations?* And there it was. For suicide, look up Psalms 143:6–11 (NASB). I thought, *Okay, I am really here and have nothing left to lose.*

> I stretch out my hands to you; my soul thirsts for you like a parched land. Selah. Answer me quickly, O Lord. My spirit fails! Hide not your face from me, lest I be like those who go down to the pit. Let me hear in the morning of your steadfast love, for in you I trust. Make me know the way I should go, for to you I lift up my soul. Deliver me from my enemies, O Lord. I have fled to you for refuge. Teach me to do your will, for you are my God! Let your good spirit lead me on level ground. For

> your sake, O Lord, preserve my life. In your righteousness bring my soul out of trouble.

As I closed the book, I took a deep breath. The fact was I was there. I was not alone. This progesterone medication I had started that week led to my inability to function or think. I took a deep breath and listened. A gentle nudge had one suggestion: to go and be among others, to not stay alone. I took it literally, and because it was almost dinnertime, I walked out to the community board area to view the menu and activities for the night. I checked in at the menu table with a couple staffers in front of the elevators, which I took as being half concierge and half guards of any escapees. I then walked over to the whiteboard filled with the weekend's activities. Art class was about to begin. I took the advice from earlier and joined in.

As I took my seat among fellow ward patients, I witnessed a vast uniqueness to every member. Ted was older, but we shared more than the same last name and initials, which made mealtime especially awkward when I would take his order instead of mine. He too had severe anxiety. Jan talked about her toxic ex who was back in the picture. Cheryl's kids checked her in for the fourth time. Keith just had his son's birth, but his anger would keep him from being able to visit. Hannah was very young to have lived through so much. Trevor survived a horrific accident and lost most all of his mind and body's function. Then there was Dan, a small man in stature with a hard heart toward anyone who spoke of religion. Cheryl prophesying didn't help any. And sweet Carol had been there for a while; in hopes of seeing her grandkids once again, she painted something for each of them. I tearfully took her lead as I poured out the blue paint for what I had hoped to be a healthy rest of our pregnancy. I hoped to one day get to meet the man journeying within me during this unfathomable time.

As I painted a little wooden horse rocker, Carol looked up. I had a feeling of her gaze on me. I was more than showing in my sixth month of pregnancy. I received so many comments of pity and sadness for my state and place of location. But Carol couldn't resist. She looked at me intently and asked, "So, are you not in your right mind?"

After the group leader rebuked her and most everyone watched, I was quiet for a moment. How did I respond without offending all those here? "Well, I think we're all abnormally normal, so yes, I guess I am out of my mind." That gave Ted a chuckle. I soon realized that I was about to form new friendships in the most unlikely of places. It wasn't those around me whom I had to worry about. Rather, those who didn't partake and insisted on isolating themselves in their rooms would be the ones most at risk. These patients would usually leave our floor escorted and forcefully medicated in the evening after refusing their treatments. The screams were enough terror to haunt us all up and down the hallways. Therefore when it was my turn to receive another progesterone dose, I refused, half afraid of being sent elsewhere. I realized that the only change over the past week to put me in this state was the medication I had started a handful of days prior. The doctor on call agreed to stop and have me monitored. Though there was a high chance of miscarriage after stopping this medication before the thirty-sixth week, I called Ken on an old-fashioned wall phone, and after praying we agreed.

Miscarriage wasn't unfamiliar to us. After losing our second pregnancy early on, there was no bigger lie that it doesn't feel real. All the hormones were well in place. And we mourned the loss of that baby. Should anything happen now, we would be taken care of. We were connected to the wing of one of the nation's top women's and children's hospitals. With a sense of uneasiness, I was told of a visitor. This late? In this weather, with such a blizzard outside? It was our church's lifegroup leader who made it a point to tell me how loved and prayed over I was. He left me with the book *Prayers That Avail Much* by Germaine Coppeland, where prayers based off of scriptures were written for most anything in life. I thanked him for bringing light into such a dark place. I read the one on peaceful sleep and went to bed. I was half afraid of the uncertainty ahead and half hopeful to realize this official psychiatric review in the morning. With that in mind, I held our baby, one arm clenched around my belly, and was able to fall asleep.

When I woke up to the reality of where I was the next morning, I looked outside. Seeing the snow blizzard in full force was even more disheartening. I missed my family and my home. I wanted nothing to do with being here any longer and was saddened to hear that the psychiatric reviews wouldn't occur until later on in the day, given the weekend's slower schedule. Therefore I went back to the advice of joining in whatever I could sign up for. After breakfast, there was group therapy and another chance at art. I half-heartedly attended both. Group wasn't as helpful as I had hoped. Our leader referenced tapping into a source—just not the source. It was a combination of meditation with trusting our animalistic instincts. I shared that any hope I received in the past was from my having accepted a savior. I let them know that I couldn't save myself, and my life depended on it.

The door opened, and the psychiatrist was finally ready for me. I quickly ran after her. She confirmed how very real my symptoms were and how often this side effect took place in expectant mothers. She also observed my mood stability returning after having had a twenty-four-hour break from this medication. But she was in no place of authority to keep me off the medication—that would be up to my obstetrician. What? The same doctor who sent me here in the first place? That removed our safety and placed us in an unnecessary state of fear. She had all the power. That was when I thought it couldn't get worse. The psychiatric evaluation was that they'd like to keep me there for another night of continued observation. There was a way out for me, and it depended on Ken agreeing to have me come home, despite their recommendations. Were they serious? I couldn't even make this decision on my own? I waited some more, knowing I had to be released into the care of another. Feeling helpless again, I returned to my room and went back to the only real source of hope that I had. I opened that little New Testament and read this big reminder:

> Let us draw near with a pure heart in full assurance of faith, with our hearts sprinkled clean from an evil conscience and our bodies washed with pure water. Let us hold fast the confession of our hope without wavering. For he who promised is faithful. And let us consider how to stir up one another to love and good works. Not neglecting to meet together, as is the habit of some, but encouraging one another, and all the more as you see the day drawing near. (Hebrews 10:22–25 NIV)

Then as if I was being spoken to, in my own voice, I heard a question. "Do you love me more than these?" *These?* I thought. *What or who are these?* Images of Ken and our two sons at home appeared. *Yes, Lord,* I replied. "Then stay another night." I knew what I had to do. Ken was as surprised as I was, but we agreed.

Before I could get into a place of self-pity, they told me

I had a visitor. Besides Ken, who could be visiting? It was my sweet friend from our lifegroup. Her smiling face, all put together, had me embarrassed to receive her visit in my frumpy state. That was when I knew we'd be friends for life—scratch that, besties. Her acceptance of me in my mess was beyond loving. She had brought me a baggie of Hershey kisses, as if her presence wasn't already the greatest gift ever. But the snow? How'd she travel in it? And she left her little son (and our toddler's best bud) and hubby at home? She only had a smile and a promise of a future girls' night once I broke free. It was just what I needed to hear. I began to feel abnormally normal again.

While at home, Ken took on the kids and the house, and he even continued to host our white elephant party with a dozen friends. Their surprise and dismay of my whereabouts would lead to continued care and concern upon my return. In that mess of our circumstances, these friends took the time to pray for our baby and me. And miraculous things began to happen.

Trying to make the best of staying another night, I took advantage of the planned activities: games and a movie night. I had formed an unusual bond among those still checked in. We could be released only into the care of someone. I thought about that. Here I am, as a mother supposed to care for others, and I was being cared for. Some of my Catholic guilt returned. A break in my mood came from the group. While playing cards, I overheard Hannah saying how it wasn't so bad. She was still able to shower, so she'd give the facility three stars. We all laughed. I didn't make it much longer after that. I tried to watch the movie but decided to try and rest.

I was awoken by the loud screams of another patient being escorted away. Where? I didn't even want to consider a place of greater isolation than here. That was when I heard someone outside my door, in the hallway. It was Dan. He was just as alarmed as I was and had left the movie. We were not allowed in each other's rooms, so he asked if I'd be willing to talk in the hallway. Both of us were in some fear, and Dan shared how he was uneasy with his roommate. Mine had checked out, so I had the room to myself. I told him that praying helped me. He asked what that might look like, so I brought out my book from my lifegroup leader and showed him the prayer written on peaceful sleep. He glanced at it and then agreed. We began to pray, reading aloud the scripture-crafted prayer. He went to his room, and I fell asleep peacefully.

The next morning, I was invigorated, mainly because I expected to return home as long as the psychiatric review went as well as the day before. Over breakfast, I sat by Dan. He was quiet, so I figured he had forgotten our conversation, especially the part about praying. After all, he was being dosed on a large amount of medications. Each morning we were called individually after breakfast to receive our meds. Mine was just a prenatal, but I took it like it was the hard stuff so I could fit in with the group. I was most surprised when Dan looked over at me and said, "I don't remember much about last night. But I do remember you praying for me. Thanks." Was this the devout atheist receiving a bit of God? I knew that if for no other reason, this horrendous stay had been worth it. God really does use everything for good, even when it doesn't feel good. And that was the lesson I brought home: that I'm not to trust my feelings—especially hormone-jacked-up, medication-induced, second-trimester ones. For that fact, not until well after the first year of birth and I stopped nursing could I begin to reason with some normal functioning. As I received clearance to return home, I decided that the little white leather-bound New Testament Bible no longer needed to be in my care. I signed it over to Dan in hopes that he would one day again see more for himself.

Returning home was just as surreal. As I placed my artwork from my weekend stay in our future son's nursery, I saw how not much was needed. To think I had made myself a home in such a stark place. So maybe home really is wherever you are. Or home is wherever He, my Savior and Lord Jesus, is. He promised to never leave us. In fact, that Good Friday in 2009, after birthing our oldest, was when His holy man was forever in this broken woman. And only He can truly ever know what I went through—not because of what had happened, but because He was also being separated from His loved one. I don't serve a God who's removed. I serve one who relates. Now, don't you think for a moment that Ken and I didn't march into that obstetrician's office together the very next day to speak some truth into her life. Truth about the hardships, not just emotionally but financially, that she had caused by not knowing her assigned hospital's procedures, leading to my weekend stay away. Yes, we spoke the truth—in love, of course.

> This day is holy to our Lord. Do not grieve, for the joy of the Lord is your strength. (Nehemiah 8:10 NIV)

Our Arrival

Spring 2017

"It could just be routine," said the midwife about my spotting. But I was in week thirty-eight with Ken flying back into town, so I figured this was it. It was time to deliver our full-term third baby boy. He was an answer to much prayer. However, that Saturday morning in late April, I would turn up to have little options of help to drive to the doctor's office. Therefore after reaching out to many friends and having sent my mom and sister-in-law off to our church's women's retreat in full assurance of all being fine, I realized it was not. I called upon that same sweet friend who had earlier in the year picked us up. She was once again back in action, swiftly relieving me of looking after our two oldest sons. I drove those twenty minutes alone with much peace to what I thought would be a simple checkup. Instead I got checked in. I didn't think there was any way that I could be four centimeters dilated. I drove while singing aloud to the tunes found on 91.9 FM WGTS, a familiar dial. It was a worship service in my van.

After parking, I left my prepacked hospital bags in the van. This was just a routine checkup, after all, I reminded myself. Our midwife's office happened to connect with the hospital where we planned to deliver our newest bundle of joy. I approached those sliding doors, and my midwife was aghast. "Who drove you?" she questioned. I told her she empowered me to take the drive alone, thinking it could just be a routine visit. We laughed it off together, and the routine exam took all of five minutes. That was when our midwife asked for my car keys to go get my hospital bag, because it was indeed time. It was also time to let the others know. I called Ken and could hear the pilot's announcements in the background because he was boarding the plane, heading home from business travels in Florida. I let him know it could be any moment now. We agreed that our midwife had told us we would have plenty of time for him to have taken this trip. That still didn't change the fact that our third son had other plans. My next call was to Ken's sister, who happened to be a nurse. She was deep into one of the women's retreat's studies when I told her it was time for Mom to relieve my friend of watching the kids, because this baby boy was making his grand debut. And because my husband and birth coach was in the air, she took me up on my request for her to fill in.

All weekend long, Ken would be known as the dad who made it. Ken arrived within the hour of our third son's birth. At one point, before he arrived, the nursing staff even laid me flat on my back to prevent any further pushing in hopes of his arrival. My new birthing coach, and this baby dad's sister, was sure to call him repeatedly, urging him to travel at a speed-breaking pace from the airport. It was all such a joy, until it wasn't. Later that evening as we got to discover this new bundle of joy, I remembered wanting nothing to do with Ken leaving the room, let alone going home to our other boys. There was a very strange attachment and safety about his presence. I tried to fix my thoughts on reading or watching whatever was available—anything to not focus on the more anxious thoughts about being left alone with my new baby. I tearfully shared with our nurse how strange I felt handling my baby when this was our third, to which she mentioned many other moms had this same tearful response. Not recognizing much of anything else, we continued as though everything was normal.

With the help of my mom, who stayed with us for a couple of months, I plugged along. Within the week, I found myself on the bathroom floor in tears over a minor argument with Ken. Feeling alone and misunderstood, I continued to push through these moments. The follow-up with our midwife did offer me support with medicine. Whether out of fear or a need to think myself stronger, I kindly refused. I did not want to lose control and be dependent on this outside support. I did agree to a postpartum support group at the hospital. What I didn't realize was that I would be alone in my beliefs and unable to pray or share my spiritual convictions in that support group. They treated only half of me, so I went just once and figured I'd be fine. I did take away learning how nearly 20 percent of new moms could have postpartum disorder, be it anxiety or depression, and 5 percent of those moms would face and detrimentally act on psychosis. As ugly as verbalizing my scary thoughts of hurting myself and baby was, I was being reassured of how this was indeed a good sign. I felt I sounded like a monster to my husband and family, but it was normal to the professionals. This sharing meant one would likely not act on one's greatest fears. I figured I learned what I needed and simply went along. However, I did turn to our church again. There would be a mom's lifegroup that would go on to pray for us with texts at any hour of the night. These prayer warriors would also love on us with meals, knowing my mom had returned to her home out west.

These moms of young children would pray for me both in our weekly morning meetings, where child care was provided, and late into the evenings when my anxieties would heighten. At one meeting, these sweet sisters in Christ laid hands on my shoulders and held my left hand. As they prayed, I sensed their warmth, and then as though one other had placed her hand in my right one, I opened my eyes. No one was visibly holding my right hand. No one had, at just the last moment, slipped it from mine. Later on that day, the one friend who had not been able to make our meeting texted her love and support, citing a scripture that took away my breath. It was found in the Old Testament book of Isaiah and spoke of God upholding me, specifically with His righteous right hand. I understood His presence to greater depths than ever before after reading this, and it would be what reassured me during what was yet to come.

> Call to me and I will answer you and tell you great and unsearchable things you do not know. (Jeremiah 33:3 NIV)

Our Home

Summer 2017

We got along at home with our family of five's new routines for a good month. We returned from a week at the beach with our family, and it was a time when I should have felt replenished. Instead I began going through the laundry mound, cleaning house for an extended family dinner, and racing around at the dollar store for school supplies to take advantage of our one-day tax-free shopping spree. I was in the checkout line with my baby, who was crying for his next meal. Then I ran home, nursed, set the table, rotated the laundry, hid the rest of the mess, and relaxed over my first glass of white pinot grigio since before the pregnancy. After dinner, I made sure to indulge in a second serving of sweets. Once all had left and our boys were resting, I got back to work. Finally I was about to call it a night when I recalled the forms I had to sign for our oldest to go to camp the next morning. I decided to sit next to Ken while he watched a show, and I began the forms.

Whether it was the scary show or my running thoughts, I began to panic. I turned to Ken and let him know I wasn't feeling well. In an instant, I was on the floor in convulsions. Ken was at a loss. What had happened to his wife, who was now incapacitated and lying in front of him? As I came to, he asked what could be done for me. In my panic, I asked that he call a friend to pray. In doing so, these same sweet, sacrificial friends showed up to our rescue again as they had so many times before. From a ride to the ill-fated hospital stay earlier in the year to the care of our older boys so I could drive to deliver our third son, these friends went from a phone prayer for an hour to an in-home call for hours. We truly felt a sort of spiritual attack and possession over my limp body, which had now been in and out of convulsions. No matter the tool, I was unable to stop this break with my reality. I would have other friends visit and do their best to make sense of this mess. Our church lifegroup leader brought some of the greatest hope. Many good-naturedly tried praying against whatever was attacking me, but this friend had me sit up and keep my gaze upward during the attacks so that my eyes stayed fixed on Jesus fixing it for me. This would come to be one of my life-saving truths.

For the next twenty-four hours, I underwent violent, seizure-like movements while screaming in terror. These attacks would last for a few minutes in hour blocks. At least four episodes later, after countless in-home visitors by our sweet church family, I'd be surrounded by the elders and head pastor of our church at my request. I talked to our head pastor prior to my in-person visit, and his counsel was to recall that the prayer of a righteous person is all that is needed. I should trust that Ken's prayers were no less powerful or mighty than his. My sister-in-law's observations when she paid us a visit also left her baffled at this surreal episode. As a psychiatric nurse, she could rule out certain diagnoses, but she also questioned the root cause of what had clearly taken hold of my physical realm. At my request, while other friends cared for our littles, she, Ken, and I left for the church to have the elders and pastor pray. We were desperate to realize the Bible's guidance to have the elders and leaders of the church pray over the sick, and they obeyed our request and prayed. In much shock, they began casting out whatever looked to be possessing the woman in front of them. What was most fearful was that as I tried to worship and sing aloud to "Amazing Grace," my body's response became more vulgar. A dozen men could not hold my thrashing body's outburst. After more than an hour of this fierce praying session, we decided to have me go home in an attempt to rest. I felt defeated after no Hollywood climax ending or removing whatever spirit was attacking me, and I fearfully tried to sleep. Any and all work or trips Ken had scheduled for the week were cleared from his calendar to take over the care of our boys and me.

When I woke the next morning, Ken informed me that we were off to see both a psychiatrist and a new counselor that our church had provided him. It just so happened that they both had openings that same day.

As I sheepishly recounted the horrors of the past twenty-four hours to this psychiatrist, I looked up and saw the most knowing of faces. He calmed me almost in an instant. He labeled me with "classic case of panic disorder with dissociative episodes of terror alongside postpartum." I thought, *Classic? That was a thing? You mean to say someone else has gone through this? I don't have to believe the lies of being a monster and living out this nightmare alone?*

To cure this, I would need both psychological and pharmaceutical help. I replied, "Anything. Sign me up. I just want to get back to my life." Ken and I began to breathe slowly again. We even stopped for a burger before the next appointment. Encouraged, I sat in front of my new Christian counselor. More relief arrived as he explained how he too had seen this state of panic in others. Then he switched hats to address the spirituality side and explained that I wasn't possessed and how it was bad theology to think otherwise. He quickly explained how no Christian could have anything but the indwelling of what is holy. His Holy Spirit cannot cohabitate with anything unholy. Attacks can still come, however this was simply a chemical imbalance. In addition to my history of anxiety and previous postpartum anxiety, I would need to learn many new self-loving and life-giving habits to survive.

This time, I gladly accepted my prescription to take 25 milligrams of Zoloft. I would slowly work myself up to what would become my set dosing of 50 milligrams daily. In a few weeks, I would get back to being myself and caring for those around me. Meanwhile, I'd still have to be monitored every other week by my psychiatrist to ensure proper dosing. Then I was seen twice a week by my counselor to help work through the psychological reasons for my state. As my counselor labeled it, "stinkin' thinkin'" was what I quickly began to identify with my postpartum anxiety, and I replaced it with biblical truth like "I praise you because I am fearfully and wonderfully made; your works are wonderful, I know that full well" (Psalm 139:14 NIV). Until my hormones balanced out chemically, my thoughts were not to be trusted. That meant more at-home days for Ken because panic still arose in those early days while I worked to gain new insights. There was certainly work to be done. I was equipped with *The Anxiety and Phobia Workbook* by Edmond J. Bourne from my counselor. I read this nightly like the Bible, because I still winced at the idea of reading my Bible so as to not invoke the same terror and panic. It was as though some form of superstition or posttraumatic stress took hold of whatever truth I tried to learn. But read it I did. I learned what a perfect storm had brewed at the onset of my panic attack. The alcohol, stress, sugars, and lack of sleep with little other self-care caused an implosion where my body had no choice but to fight back by fleeing from itself.

I'd go on to take surveys in this workbook regarding

just how many stressors were already in my life. Even good things like having a baby and vacation can still cause stress. For every major life event, whether or not you handle change well, it will still manifest in your body somehow. What I had suppressed simply resurfaced. Each night around 9:00 p.m., I'd discipline myself over a cup of hot chamomile and this workbook, learning until I was too weary to go on. That meant no more late-night screens and shows that had connected Ken and me as us time. Amazingly, I had better rest when I went to bed earlier. I also learned about the family history of stress being carried down by generations. My DNA could be made up of more anxious genes than another. Early to bed was just one of the many nonnegotiable routines I would begin to set for myself. Our human bodies truly thrive on routine. Some are more destructive than others, and the recent episodes played in my mind as the driving force to create new habits that would become a new way of living.

Once I learned about bedtime, next came a focus on exercise and nutrition. What you eat is what you are, and your body pangs to move and remove excess energy daily. This meant avoiding stimulants like caffeine and depressants like alcohol. I infused my body with things that lived in the fridge instead of the easy pantry options. I had no choice but to slow down and start seeing more for my self-care. I had heard all my life that to care for others, one had to care for oneself first. As a mother of three young boys, I thought it almost frivolous to stop for myself. I was driven to push through any thoughts of a break, and my body showed me otherwise and broke. Here I was, left with nothing to give, and I could only receive to be restored. I would receive a slow uptake in medications for a hopeful chemical balance. I received sound advice and heeded it. I received the help of Ken taking over. I received the meals, the breaks, and the love. It was an outpouring of protection over our family as I sought to receive my health again. I would receive more than this one part of my being. I'd receive complete restoration.

> Resist him, standing firm in the faith, because you know that the family of believers throughout the world is undergoing the same kind of sufferings. And the God of all grace, who called you to his eternal glory in Christ, after you have suffered a little while, will himself restore you and make you strong, firm and steadfast. (1 Peter 5:9–10 NIV)

Our Family

Spring 2018

Even after all of these great tools and steps, more panic returned. The next feat was to set boundaries. What fueled my anxiety was a lack of boundaries. Therefore my communication was not assertive. Instead, it was passive on good days and aggressive on bad days. My counselor had to work with me on naming it. Past hurts that I let build into resentment were cured only by speaking up. Whether it was in my marriage, with extended family, or with my parents while growing up, I began to realize all the people-pleasing, selfish, victim-mode ways of thinking kept me quiet most days and anxious the rest of the time.

It was when I sat on the couch in my dear friend's home that this new panic arose. And again, it was during the most unlikely of times: while in group prayer. Our littles were sent down to the basement so as to not witness such strange and scary convulsions, and I lay there in fear of never shaking this state. Their prayers were sweet and swift, strong and sound, so much so that I realized I hadn't eaten enough and needed some sugar. My body's sugars stabilized enough to have me sit up and find some rest again. A sweet friend took me and our two younger sons home. It was there, back at home, where she would go on to witness even more panic. I entered the house to the sound of our oldest being cared for by my brother-in-law's sweet wife yet again. As a former preschool director, her joyful presence was truly serving as another mother to our sons during every doctor visit that took me away, leaving me such peace. As my friend swiftly explained to her the need to wait for Ken's return home given another onset of an attack, my friend began to care for me in our half bath downstairs.

This sweet friend and momma to her own three kiddos would stay with me on that linoleum floor and pray until the episode subsided. While we waited, she asked if there was anything I knew to be especially helpful. I simply asked to be distracted while it overtook my body. She grabbed her smartphone and began to play us some music and even a comedy skit. She told me of her own life and apologized for not understanding how to better help me. I could then share how all that was required was the presence of a willing and caring soul. This gift went straight into my bones bringing me great cheer. Once the panic passed and our kids' sweet aunt walked home—I was grateful for the day I moved into the house a block over that she also discovered for us—my friend departed when Ken was back home. I was unable to understand why I still suffered these more minor attacks after doing all the right things according to the experts, but I began to do the hardest work of my life: speaking up for myself.

As a result of this newer work and my speaking up, our marriage would have to undergo another harsh trial. My counselor advised marriage counseling to help with my ability to communicate assertively and in love. After arriving late to that first session, Ken was quickly addressed by our counselor as his forgetting. He refuted that and said he simply got detained and carried away in another conversation. The counselor once again clarified how that was forgetting. This was the beginning of our continued rough restart. In retrospect, an independent counselor separate from my personal sessions would have made for a better start. Ken, who had been the rock in caring for us all, was now being asked to admit to his own faults. That required him to question and identify changes he may have to make. To say the least, it was our first and last meeting as a couple. I threatened to walk out on the session halfway through it and was talked down by the counselor to reconsider, because this would only confirm Ken's observations. We at least agreed to do the counselor's ten-minute check-in nightly as our homework. This would be where, without interruption, we checked in with one another. It required asking the other person to share something newsworthy about their day, a bite-sized complaint, a compliment and a future goal. This would continue for a while, but most definitely it did not happen the night of our silent treatment.

The next day had me in a private session with the counselor. I half expected a talk about my behavior, but I was asked how long I had been under his paternal role. Shocked and surprised, I began to realize to no one's fault, including Ken's, I was unable to make a decision for myself. Many of my life's decisions came out of seeking others' approval. This sense of belonging had made me blind to any of my true desires, needs, or wants. To know myself meant to spend time knowing who made me.

Therefore I arose one Saturday with a determination to have intentional quiet time after feeding the masses. I went into our room in private and began to sing again, to worship. I sang a song that had me saying "beautiful Jesus" over and over, and I started to shake. Worried that another attack was resurfacing, I heard it again. Rather, I heard Him in my own voice. I knew I could never ask myself these questions. "Do you want to be healed?" Of course I wanted to be done with the anxiety. Why would that be a question? Then I rethought how I was holding on to anxiety as a form of my identity. In that moment, I said, "Yes, I want to be healed." I began to have convulsions, and for a moment I was saddened at what the past had shown in these moments to be true, but then I realized I was still standing. I had not gone to the floor helplessly. And right there, in an audible response, I yelled, "Jehovah Rapha" (the God who heals). Then it stopped. I wasn't shaking. I wasn't yelling. I was simply sitting in awe.

That was when I offered my thanks. I knew I was healed from anxiety. I heard, "Then stop your meds." What? Stop one of the major reasons I could now function these days? This would certainly prove whether my anxiety had left for good or not, but I thought again. This time, I prayed, "If this is of You, God, keep the thought of my stopping the meds coming. If not, take it away."

A response was given right away, and again in my own voice but certainly not a thought I could muster: "These meds are a part of your journey. Do not stop them."

I painfully began to speak up. Most days, I still had a short fuse and was very reactionary. Some days, I had a calm and collected presence that had me wondering who I was. It was during this time that I came to realize the need for healthy boundaries with our extended family and friends. Our immediate family as wife, husband, and three sons was blurred with extended family, neighbors, and friends' needs. We were quick to overextend our schedules and tempers in hopes to gain the approval and affirmation of those around us, but not with each other. After having already done so much, this was hard to say and even harder to hear for Ken. What amazed me was the calm and sure stance I kept in requesting that he make us his first priority outside of God.

After having walked away hurt, and not wanting to reopen that wound, Ken agreed to discuss what these boundaries meant another time. I was able to clarify how I appreciated all he did and that we would institute time away from each other too. Each week, he would have a night off from us, and so would I. We could use this time to take a class, visit friends, or do whatever we wanted. Then once a week, we would take a night for each other without the kids. And once the kids were in bed, that meant we could quickly reconnect before going on with a show or book, or visit with other family and friends. We both agreed to recommit to our family, placing aside resentment harbored for the recent hardships that had disrupted our family norms. Over time and with practice, we began to make the other a priority. In our sacrifice of self, we could better serve one another and these boys. This recommitment was our family's new start, with both parents' actively choosing each other.

> He tends his flock like a shepherd: He gathers the lambs in his arms and carries them close to his heart; he gently leads those that have young. (Isaiah 40:11 NIV)

Our Joy

Fall 2019

In an effort to recommit, I brought up a request to Ken to renew our vows. It was a sort of reproposal to him that would involve our sons. I had struggled as newlyweds with my more passive, pleasing role as a bride. I wanted to show our three sons the value and joy in our family. I would get to travel with Ken for work to Florida earlier in the year thanks to Mom's trip out to care for our sons, so he questioned my need for yet another getaway. In my mind, this would mark a renewal of God's goodness and my having remained panic free. Ken was able to transform his resentment of our recent history into a real-life application with a troubled coworker. God had given him a way to approach and relate to this young man with a gentle, knowing spirit—one he would not have had if it weren't for our recent events riddled in panic. Strangely, all these hardships did make us stronger. We were less fearful and more trusting.

Ken once again trusted in my being led to renew our vows. We would bring our boys, my bestie and her family, to officiate and to capture the moment, along with our "adopted" daughter. Our former neighbor and sitter had turned into the daughter we never had. Both her and my bestie had event skills, so they would pull off an intimate setting where I had chosen to have us go: beachside. This time I paid for the dress! I even had it tailored to my exact liking. It is the very one featured on this book's back cover. This simple act was tremendous for me—to pay the price of what I felt joyful wearing. The bonus and God's grace was finding the dress on clearance. In the past, this would have been a frivolous pursuit. I now understood it to be one of abundant living, a promise our good God promotes.

His promises do come true. We would have to reschedule our trip due to a hurricane's devastation. Understanding why we could no longer go beachside, and in refusal to postpone until April 2020 for our sixteenth anniversary, God knew better by redirecting us inland and on marshland. Near the border of South Carolina was where we would now celebrate this exchange. When I sat to write out my vows to him, I was amazed that they were also to Him, my rescuer. The following thoughts that I would come to share with Ken are many of those I shared in these pages. They would serve as my renewal to our covenant between God and us.

- Rescuer.

  - ❖ When I met you eighteen years ago, besides taking my breath away with your golden locks and that deep echo of a voice, I kept myself from thinking much of anything would come of it.
  - ❖ When you met every single one of the items I had listed in a perfect mate after my first heartache, I still thought it a distant dream to think of us together forever.

- Something changed.

  - ❖ As you invited me to paradise not just in my mind but to our first home church together, where we would be married only a few years later, I went and kept going.

- ❖ As an only child, and one too many Disney fairytales later, I believed you were starting to become my knight in shining armor, my rescuer.
- ❖ Then when you invited me to coffee to do a bible study together, I went and kept reading. Like a child, I could not get enough of this Word.
- ❖ When you asked me to marry you on that pier, I knew my happily ever after had arrived.

- So why did I struggle?

  - ❖ First with insecurity over my health, my career, and our wealth.
  - ❖ Then in breaking ties as an only child from all that I had known.
  - ❖ In that flight where I thought our baby was leaving us, and you asked me to pray.
  - ❖ The day we did lose our second baby to a better home, unsure of ever giving our then only son a sibling.

- You still led.

  - ❖ When I thought we lost so much in this world, we still read His Word. Still prayed. Still loved.
  - ❖ Soon, a brother was born.
  - ❖ Then those two became big brothers to yet another son.
  - ❖ Soon we had a bigger family by growing where He planted us. Our family stands with us today to witness where we are now.

    - Even after having more recent struggles and still greater joys, they can see what I've seen all this time.

- A Godly man.

    - A man who knows where his happiness is rooted.
    - A man who looks up to His rescuer.
    - And on this day, I too look up to my one true rescuer. The one who rescued me from so many poor choices in my past. To my one true love who would guide me into His happily forever arms alongside you, my love.

- Now, I am a child of God.

    - I am a child of our Rescuer because of you Ken.
    - I am thankful for the Son, who blessed us with our three sons.
    - Now these sons look to their father, who guides them to the only Father worth knowing.

I finished with, "Because God joined us together, I will follow you wherever you go. I love you, Ken!" I thanked him for living out His Word, as it is written in the book of Ephesians: "Be completely humble and gentle; be patient, bearing with one another in love. Make every effort to keep the unity of the Spirit through the bond of peace" (Ephesians 4:2–3 NIV).

This exchange of our vows would end with our boys coming together and pouring their own colored sand into a decorated mason jar. More than a keepsake, it was a teaching to our boys to always see what they would come to appreciate in their future loves. It didn't hurt that as a family with our friends, we took a drive south to enjoy a second honeymoon at Disney World. With joy, we bounded to our grand adventures among friends: the wilderness lodge to play and splash around a poolside, or our daily boat rides into magical kingdoms. We discovered new lands that had just been created, and we caught the joy of our oldest as he entered into his own personal Star Wars World while boarding the Millennium Falcon. Our youngest fought off monsters in his saucer cup with Buzz Lightyear while our middle son and his best friend got to walk behind the scenes and see the inner workings of a rollercoaster after braving a wild ride, only to get stuck midway. Our sweet "adopted" daughter gifted us with a double date out in Epcot so Ken and I could taste our way around the world with friends. These were just a few of the many joyful moments we received. We were completely unaware of what the following year would bring. Our family would receive more than we could have asked. Joy.

We both had to actively choose to follow His joy in our newfound routines and the life we had built together. We were able to see His joy replacing whatever obedience we attempted to muster up in the past. With time, we reconciled to more than just our marriage and family. We came home to the one who was waiting all along for us to follow His joy.

> I have told you this so that my joy may be in you and that your joy may be complete. (John 15:11 NIV)

Your Story Here

A few years past the onset of my first dissociative panic attack due to anxiety, there have been none further. Unbelievably, I became a graduate of therapy and psychiatry! The counseling ended a year prior to the continued psychiatric support, and given my history with multiple anxiety episodes of panic attacks, I was monitored for longer and continued another year of medicating. Thinking back on when I began seeing a counselor, never did I consider an end to it all. Changing counselors and taking breaks was as much of a stop as I thought possible. For a counselor to declare my departure from him completely was a total novelty. He reminded me that though his services remained an option, he no longer saw the need to see me any further. I had been tested and tried. I had set boundaries and painted those fences. My consistent new lifestyle of God care, self-care, and other care proved to be successful. I had returned, and for the first time I ran my day-to-day life joyfully as a mom to these three brave boys.

Counseling gave me a voice I did not have before. As a people pleaser to the core, I made it my mission to make all those around me as content as I could. I dodged conflict to keep the peace. There were no borders, let alone healthy boundaries. Therefore I slowly asked for what I needed, or even at times what I wanted. It felt selfish, but that was far from the truth. I now see how I was playing the role of victim, and that was selfish. It is not really humble when you lose it with those you love most due to not loving yourself. I addressed things like sleep, quiet time, exercise, diet, and even extended family and friends. I made a consistent schedule to rest and rise around the same time. We knew every step counted, so we simply started walking. I got rid of "all or nothing" thinking. I rose to have quiet time with my real source of energy and purpose. I took care to stop the excess sweets, drink more water, and watch any alcohol. I talked with Ken about how to love our immediate family first and then reach out from there. It would make for some hard talks when we put up new routines. My night away from the kids. Then his. Then ours. Weekly. All of this would pay off over the years, and I continue to remain set free from anxiety.

I don't know the details of your seasons, but I am in a relationship with one who does. And I pray you are too. If not, what's holding you back from getting to know this loving Savior? There is no denying that for my story, He has rescued me from anxiety, depression, postpartum, panic disorder, lack of boundaries, and financial hardships, among other life-changing events. The life-saving event He has already done for me and for you is His greatest rescue of all. This rescuer stands at the door of your heart, knocking and asking to come and stay forever. There is no need to get ready. Work harder. Change first. Give your honest yes. "Yes, I get that I need help. Yes, please forgive me. Yes, I see you now for the Son of God who gave it all for me. Yes, I want to be with You always. Yes, I'll accept Your help right now and forevermore. Yes, I will walk into the mansion You've gone ahead of me to prepare for each of us. Yes, I will sing of Your goodness all the days of my life. Yes."

For those who say yes, I now leave you with the same

challenge that was given to me when I chose to say yes in writing to you. Ask Jesus and the Holy Spirit to "speak LORD, for your servant is listening" (1 Samuel 3:10 NIV). Write down whatever comes to mind. Nothing is too revealing, too out there, too much for the one who knows and loves you completely. Then ask again for Him to confirm His message. Next is your choice to obey and watch Him at work in you. It won't be easy. Or it might be. Whatever it is, it is yours to tell, to share, and to help those who will also come alongside your rescuing truth.

> And they overcame him because of the blood of the Lamb and because of the word of their testimony. (Revelation 12:11 NASB)

Your Story

PGIL2021USA